Ententes Cordiales

Ententes Cordiales

The French in London & other adventures

By David Arkell

Illustrated by Philip Norman

Foreword ~ Claire Tomalin

First published in Great Britain in 1989 by
Carcanet Press
208–212 Corn Exchange Buildings
Manchester M4 3BQ

British Library Cataloguing in Publication Data
Arkell, David
   Ententes Cordiales.
   1.   Title
   828' . 91407

ISBN 0-85635-791-X

The publisher acknowledges the financial assistance of the
Arts Council of Great Britain.

Printed in England by SRP Ltd, Exeter.

CONTENTS

Foreword by Claire Tomalin

Part One: THE FRENCH IN LONDON

Part Two: OTHER ADVENTURES

Claire Tomalin

Foreword

David Arkell is one of those rare, congenial writers blessed with the ability to set his readers down in a vanished landscape and allow them to see and understand whatever was going on there. It is often something small, always something telling. Like the best magicians, he makes the process of transporting us seem quite effortless. As the title he has given this collection of essays suggests, its theme is the relations between French and English: *Ententes*, usually if not always *Cordiales*. The first half of the book is devoted to French visitors to England; those poets, painters and novelists of the 19th and 20th centuries who were attracted by the fog and grey skies ('as if God couldn't see you' said Mallarmé); by the much-admired Anglo-Saxon sporting life; by pretty English *demoiselles* – the poet Jules Laforgue said there were three sexes, men, women and English girls – and strong-minded English landladies; by the gaiety, squalor and exoticism of the great city on the Thames.

The second half of the book ranges more widely, although it is still anchored quite firmly in the world of Anglo-French relations. This special corner of cultural history is one to which Mr Arkell has made a notable contribution over the years. He is not an academic but an enthusiast whose love of his subject has made him at least as learned as most academics; yet he is never dry or pompous, and there is not a word of jargon in his vocabulary.

One of Mr Arkell's skills is to write about his subjects as

7

The Reading Room
British Museum

though they were friends he has just run into at the corner pub – or café: friends who may make him smile, may tug at his heartstrings, friends who are never dull company. Here is Upper Norwood, and here is Emile Zola, disguised in a bowler hat and pince-nez, carefully counting the hairpins dropped on the pavement by the suburban nursemaids, as part of the research for his naturalistic novel *Fécondité*, due to be finished and published the following year, 1899. How solid and serious Zola seems, although he is in fact in flight from imprisonment in France (for libelling the General Staff) and about to be joined, at the Queen's Hotel, Church Road, Crystal Palace, by his pretty young mistress and their two children. He is engaged in a political flight, and a piece of literary labour, yes; but it is also a delicious holiday jaunt, all among the Norwood nursemaids' hairpins.

Here too is Willingham, the white-haired St John's Wood gardener, posing for the happy, respectable domestic scenes painted by his French employer, Tissot, in the garden of 44 Grove End Road; but things are neither so respectable nor so happy as they seem in this household of the 1870s. Later, in the same garden, Willingham is observed burning the bedding of Kathleen Newton, Tissot's mistress, dead at 28 of tuberculosis; and Tissot leaves St John's Wood, and England, for good.

Here are two distinguished men of letters, Alphonse Daudet and George Meredith, embracing politely as they say farewell on the platform at Box Hill, and unfortunately unable to disentangle themselves as the train gets up steam: Meredith is carried along the platform with his legs in the air.

Here are the mean streets of Stepney at the turn of the century, where young Louis Hémon elects to settle, away from his prosperous and conventional French family; he attends boxing matches in the Whitechapel Road and sends sporting articles to *Le Vélo* and *L'Auto*; he also fathers a daughter on an Irish girl, Lydia O'Kelly, who goes mad. Hémon leaves for Canada, where he writes *Maria Chapdelaine*, which will become a triumphant bestseller. But he falls under a train before it is even published.

There is nothing hazy or impressionistic about these glimpses of other times and other lives; each is as bright and sharp as a new coin. David Arkell is a fine writer, but it is the discovery of facts that delights him; the charm of anecdote is always backed by serious scholarship. He is a born researcher, clearly revelling in its private eye aspects, the trails through registers of births and deaths, rate books and old newspaper columns, the time-devouring correspondence, the exchanges of photocopies and discoveries of blurred, poignant snapshots, the correlating of one bit of information culled from a memoir with another found in a newly discovered collection of tattered letters, the conversations with strangers that establish where a house once stood, or a street once ran. At all this he is expert; and he appears to know the British Library catalogues as well as his own library. He is also unfailingly generous with his knowledge and expertise when others ask him for assistance; obsessed with following faint trails himself, he understands the obsessions of fellow-workers and is always ready to lend a hand.

The most famous and thrilling of his discoveries is set out here in a classic essay called 'Looking for Leah Lee'. In it he describes his long search for the origins of the English wife of the poet Jules Laforgue. His success provided a crowning achievement for a justly celebrated biography; it also casts interesting light on our preconceptions about the ways of provincial Victorian girls. Leah, born in 1861, was one of sixteen children of a Teignmouth draper; when her widowed father displeased her by marrying the governess in charge of her younger siblings, she took herself boldly off to the continent to study, and in Germany she met Laforgue, young, already ill, penniless and a genius. They married, without parental blessing, in London in 1886. Within two years first he and then she were dead of tuberculosis. She was wise enough to preserve every scrap of his work but modestly destroyed her own letters: a sad loss, for she was clearly a spirited and remarkable young woman.

Arkell has specialized in Anglophile Frenchmen, perhaps because he is himself a passionately Francophile Englishman. 'I don't suppose anyone appreciates the south of France as much as an Englishman on the morning of his arrival. From the moment your bare feet touch the tiled floor of your bedroom and you hear the tinny sound of church bells your heart feels somehow lighter,' he writes in 'Tale of a Tree', in the second section of this book, which contains several such glimpses of his own experience as one living between two well loved cultures, and nourished by both. How perfectly he catches that vanishing south of France: the floor tiles – hexagonal *terre cuite*, often loosely set so that they rattled – and the tinny bells are both less in evidence than they were. At least Arkell has captured them for ever.

There is a literal, geographical background to this duality of his. His grandparents were Channel Islanders from Jersey. His grandfather played the organ at St Helier cathedral, and is reputed to have known Lily Langtry. His mother and uncle were educated as much in France as in England; Uncle Teddy, otherwise known as Edwin Evans, became a music critic and friend of Diaghilev, Stravinsky, Poulenc and Picasso – a good sort of uncle for a boy with eyes and ears alert to music, pictures and ballet.

The young David was taken to France regularly, and sent off on his own to stay with a French family at the age of fourteen. In 1935 he was living in Paris, and working as a sub-editor for the Continental Daily Mail. When the war came he attempted to leave for England on a bicycle, but was caught by the Germans before he reached the Breton coast and sent back, a civilian internee, for four years' dreary imprisonment in St Denis. There he remained until the liberation of Paris. What did you do during the four years, I asked him. Walked round and round, as prisoners do, was his answer.

His life has not been without tragedy: which may have helped to quicken his response to the men and women he writes about with such generous humanity. Some are famous, some obscure, but all emerge in these pages as abundantly alive. *Ententes Cordiales* is a book with a special flavour – *un parfum particulier* – which will find many devotees, and be enjoyed as much for the personality of its author as for the touching, funny, surprising and absorbing stories it has to tell.

The French in London

Mallarmé

The Poet of the Trocadero

hen Stéphane Mallarmé came to London in November 1862 he lodged in a secluded square not a hundred yards from Piccadilly Circus. No such square exists today but those who wish to pay their respects to the French poet may visit the escalators at the heart of the Trocadero leisure complex between Shaftsbury Avenue and Coventry Street: they will at that point be standing exactly on the site of old Panton Square.

'We are living in a square off Coventry Street,' wrote the twenty year old Mallarmé to his friend Henri Cazalis. 'London's but a step away yet here I'm in the country. Not so much as a cat around but – to make up for it – we're visited by hurdy-gurdies, monkeys in red caps, banjo-strumming blacks and Lancashire street-bands. Punch himself puts on a daily show and I love it. Marie, on the other hand, considers herself far too sensible and grown-up to enjoy Punch, and I scold her for that.'

Marie Gerhard was his German girl-friend, with whom he had run away secretly to London and was living 'on the second floor of paradise' at 9 Panton Square. But this same letter hints at trouble to come, for he reports a visit *alone* to Henri's English *inamorata* Ettie Yapp. On this and all following occasions Marie had to be left behind, and she didn't like it. 'I saw a chocolate-coloured omnibus bound for Chelsea and I scampered after it,' says Mallarmé. 'In less than an hour I was at 3 Royal Avenue Terrace. Mr Yapp was out but I stayed and talked to Mrs Yapp and managed to slip your note to Ettie, who took it delicately like a kiss. Whenever the conversation drifted along other channels she always brought it deftly back to Monsieur Cazalis.'

Ettie was the daughter of the *Daily Telegraph* correspondent in Paris, and herself a budding journalist. Completely bilingual and a vibrant seventeen (ten years younger than Marie) she impressed Mallarmé: he visited her three times in the first week, each time reminding himself that she was the friend of a friend and therefore out of bounds. If he was careful to hide the existence of Marie back in Panton Square he had a good excuse: the liaison would have been frowned on by the Yapps and might have reflected badly on Henri.

A day or two after his arrival Mallarmé had been swindled out of some cash, and he felt all the more hard done by when the authorities told him that it was his own silly fault. But a little thing like that couldn't change his mind about London: he even liked our grey skies, they made everything seem so private and cosy. 'As if God couldn't see you,' was the way he put it. In his next letter he returns to the scene below him in Panton Square. It is late in the evening: 'I've just thrown a sou to some poor lamenting hurdy-gurdy. The time's ten o'clock and its owner probably hasn't eaten yet. He'll be counting on this particular Marseillaise for his next penn'orth of bread. How sad the closed windows, curtained and shuttered, must seem! It's one thing to play for a lighted house, glowing with life and kindness within – but what must it be like to churn away below a row of dark rectangles, as indifferent as the wall itself? Marie says the man's a useless idler and that there are lots of poor people more deserving of our pennies. Useless? Surely not. Making music in the streets is a job like any other, and if it's useless so much the better. Could there be a more beautiful life than to wander the streets dispensing sad and gay tunes? Never knowing who's going to appear: angel or harridan. Playing for the sparrows and the cobblestones and the shabby trees. They're strolling poets, those people: even if the instrument is grotesque the intention's sublime. I explain all this to Marie, who doesn't seem convinced. She's half asleep and, pouring the ale just now, she missed my glass. She says goodnight to you.'

Marie was fed up. In a note ·to Henri she says: 'I must confess to you, Monsieur Cazalis, that I'll never get used to these dark, sad clouds and terrible fog. Yesterday it was so thick again that we had the lamp on all day. It creeps in the window and suffocates you.' Mallarmé, on the other hand, loved the fog and when the summer eventually came and they were living in South Kensington he wondered what was wrong. In July he wrote: 'I hate London without the fog.'

So long as they were at Panton Square, Marie was more or less marooned, sleazy Coventry Street at the end of the alley being no place for a respectable woman. She braved it with Mallarmé for their daily walks to St James's Park, but she never got used to the swarming pimps and prostitutes. In nine months she twice ran away, once to Paris and again to Brussels.

Yet on 10 August 1863 Marie and Mallarmé were married at Brompton Oratory and returned to Paris to lead such a long and happy life together that it became legendary. Henri Cazalis, for his part, jilted Ettie Yapp, whose short life was far from happy. Under the name of Eliane de Marsy she wrote a long series of Paris Letters for the London *Queen*. Her descriptions of the last days of the Second Empire were especially praised. She even became a war correspondent during the Siege of Paris (1870–1), sending her reports out by balloon, but on 10 September 1873 she died in childbirth: she was 27.

The Phantom Puff-Puff of Penge

A refugee from the Franco-Prussian War, Camille Pissarro came to London in the autumn of 1870 with Julie Vellay and the two children, Lucien and Jeanne. By the time he left in June of the next year he had painted a dozen important landscapes; and he had married Julie at Croydon Registry Office. Altogether he was well pleased with the way things had turned out. 'Monet and I were very enthusiastic about the London landscapes. Monet worked in the parks while I studied the effects of mist, snow and springtime in Upper Norwood.'

One of the springtime pictures was the famous 'Penge Station' (now in the Courtauld Institute Gallery) which shows a small steam train approaching round a gentle curve in the track. Behind the train on the right is a miniature railway station and, to the left, some distant houses, notably a bulky semi-detached pair apparently made of Lego.

Like many Frenchmen Pissarro treated all things Anglo-Saxon in a fairly cavalier fashion, and it became clear some years ago that the title of the picture was a typical Gallic cock-up; whatever it represented it had nothing to do with Penge. Thanks to some brilliant detective work by Martin Reid in the *Burlington Magazine* (April 1977) the real subject was found to be situated one and a half miles farther north, the station in question being Lordship Lane, East Dulwich. The station no longer exists; neither does the railway. Still standing, however, are the two chunky semi-detached houses on the left of picture: numbers 563-5 Lordship Lane. Also extant is the footbridge from which the picture was painted.

The *naïf* style of the painting suggests that the train, station and houses are bunched close together. In reality the train would have been 100 yards away from the artist on the bridge, with the station 250 yards away on the right, and the distant houses 400 yards on left. I have to be precise because visitors going to the spot today will need all the help available. From the bridge they will be confronted with a sheer wall of vegetation, the track and the cutting itself having vanished under a massive intrusion of trees and bushes. The little train, if it ran today, would be swallowed up in dense undergrowth long before it reached the bridge.

Ah, the bridge! That bridge was certainly built to last and is probably good for another thousand years. It is a Victorian branch-line version of the Bridge on the River Kwai, constructed of iron, stone and wood on two brick arches. The Crystal Palace and South London Junction Railway didn't do things by halves in 1865.

While waiting on the bridge for the train that would never come, I met a lady from Dulwich whose husband had travelled the line in his youth. It had closed down, she told me, in September 1954, and the station had disappeared soon afterwards. 'But that little path over there probably leads down to what was the station yard.' (The path in question is also just visible on the right of Pissarro's picture.) It seemed that the rot had really set in with the 1936 fire that destroyed Crystal Palace. After that there was no good reason for the old CP & SLJ Railway to keep going.

I walked away feeling a little sad. But the expedition ended happily in a way that might have pleased Pissarro. The whole site today has become part of a nature reserve called Sydenham Hill Wood, a jewel in the crown of the London Wildlife Trust. Before I left I met a young man in jeans who seemed so pleased with his lot that he couldn't help telling me why: he had just been appointed warden of the place. To think (he said) that he might still be working in an office. He could hardly believe his luck.

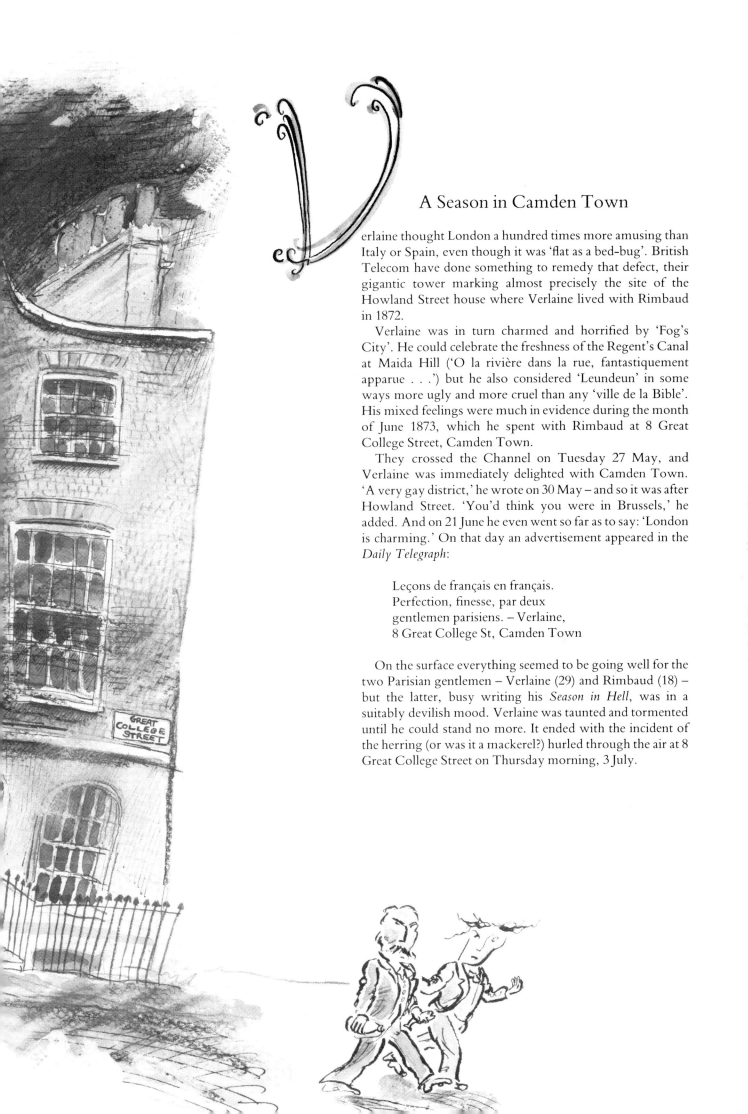

A Season in Camden Town

Verlaine thought London a hundred times more amusing than Italy or Spain, even though it was 'flat as a bed-bug'. British Telecom have done something to remedy that defect, their gigantic tower marking almost precisely the site of the Howland Street house where Verlaine lived with Rimbaud in 1872.

Verlaine was in turn charmed and horrified by 'Fog's City'. He could celebrate the freshness of the Regent's Canal at Maida Hill ('O la rivière dans la rue, fantastiquement apparue . . .') but he also considered 'Leundeun' in some ways more ugly and more cruel than any 'ville de la Bible'. His mixed feelings were much in evidence during the month of June 1873, which he spent with Rimbaud at 8 Great College Street, Camden Town.

They crossed the Channel on Tuesday 27 May, and Verlaine was immediately delighted with Camden Town. 'A very gay district,' he wrote on 30 May – and so it was after Howland Street. 'You'd think you were in Brussels,' he added. And on 21 June he even went so far as to say: 'London is charming.' On that day an advertisement appeared in the *Daily Telegraph*:

> Leçons de français en français.
> Perfection, finesse, par deux
> gentlemen parisiens. – Verlaine,
> 8 Great College St, Camden Town

On the surface everything seemed to be going well for the two Parisian gentlemen – Verlaine (29) and Rimbaud (18) – but the latter, busy writing his *Season in Hell*, was in a suitably devilish mood. Verlaine was taunted and tormented until he could stand no more. It ended with the incident of the herring (or was it a mackerel?) hurled through the air at 8 Great College Street on Thursday morning, 3 July.

Verlaine had been doing the shopping (it was Rimbaud's turn to tidy the room) and was returning down Plender Street with the herring in one hand, a bottle of oil in the other. Rimbaud, watching at the open window, saw Verlaine a long way off as he walked down the middle of the wide street with his fish and his oil. As he drew near, the younger man, elegantly propped against the window, called out: 'If you could only see what a clot you look!' Verlaine burst up the stairs, threw the fish at his friend (but not, fortunately, the bottle) and immediately began to pack.

Soon he was striding towards St Katharine's Dock to catch the next boat for Belgium, while Rimbaud hurried after pleading with him not to go. Even when Verlaine was safely aboard with the gangplank up, Rimbaud still cried out from the quayside, begging him not to leave a poor compatriot stranded in the big city. But Verlaine for once was adamant and the ship bore him away down the Thames.

Rimbaud returned to 8 Great College Street in tears and sought consolation from the landlady, Mrs Alexander Smith. A hectic exchange of letters then followed, ending with a telegram from Verlaine on Tuesday 8 July to say he was joining the Spanish Army. This was too much for Rimbaud – he said goodbye to Mrs Smith and caught a boat for Antwerp after pawning two pairs of Verlaine's trousers to pay for the ticket. Unfortunately, in the rush to save his friend from a glorious death in Spain, he forgot to take Verlaine's laundry and some other possessions left at Great College Street. Verlaine was peeved and wrote to Mrs Smith in English as follows:-

Madam, I will return to day in Paris, rue de Lyon, 12. Do you please (as soon as possible) send to me in my box all things wich remain in the room again.
        Yours obedient servant
            P.V.
I will send to you the money for expedition immediately after receiving my goods at the adress above written.

We do not know if Mrs Smith sent the box, or even understood the request. In any case Verlaine did not go to Paris. He was detained in Belgian prisons for the next eighteen months for shooting and wounding the aforesaid M. Rimbaud. 8 Great College Street today bears no marks of those goings-on. Indeed, it is now *Royal* College Street, and if it still remembers the two crazy Frenchmen and their season in Camden Town, it does so with dignity – and a rather handsome plaque.

Villiers Comes to Town

ne of the splendid asides in *Flaubert's Parrot* concerns the visit to London of Villiers de l'Isle-Adam. But Julian Barnes devoted a mere paragraph to the episode. We may perhaps be allowed here to give it a little more body. After all, nothing should be skimped in the presentation of that great aristocrat of letters, the Comte de Villiers.

Here is the story as told (page 42) by Barnes: 'Villiers de l'Isle-Adam, chronically poor yet crazily practical, came over in search of an heiress. A Parisian marriage-broker had kitted him out for the expedition with a fur overcoat, a repeating alarm watch and a new set of false teeth, all to be paid for when the writer landed the heiress's dowry. But Villiers, tirelessly accident-prone, botched the wooing. The heiress rejected him, the broker turned up to reclaim the coat and the watch, and the discarded suitor was left adrift in London, full of teeth but penniless.'

There were elements in this account that puzzled and intrigued me. What was a repeating alarm watch? Why had the marriage-broker shown such compassion in leaving Villiers his teeth? It was clearly a case to be pursued at the British Library.

First, the watch: a repeater strikes again the *previous* hour at the touch of a spring. The value of this to Villiers was obvious: if he was in an amorous daze he could at least hear the hour it had lately been. But the broker's pity was a more complex question, which entailed my going deep into the Villiers file.

I was lucky to find the book I needed: A. W. Raitt's 1981 biography, in which the incident is set out (pages 138-45) with a nice sense of irony. The marriage-broker turns out to be one Comte de La Houssaye, and who better to help a Comte than another Comte? The famous overcoat was actually fur-*trimmed*, a style that Villiers affected all his life. The watch, coat and teeth, however, were not the only preparations. Villiers also took English lessons with his dear friend Mallarmé, who conveniently happened to teach English in a Paris lycée. It was a crash course, consisting of two lessons . . . and two (unspecified) verbs.

Raitt describes the contract between the two Comtes as 'one of the most incredible pacts since Faust's agreement with Mephistopheles'. Dated 23 December 1873, it provided that Villiers should pay La Houssaye 200,000 frs – but only if the marriage materialized. It also stipulated that 'the fortune of the wife of the Comte de Villiers shall amount to at least three millions'.

With these preliminaries out of the way Villiers travelled to England at the end of December and clocked in at the Grosvenor Hotel, Victoria. The idyll got off to a flying start: the lady (an Irish girl called Anna Eyre) had been brought up in Paris and desired nothing more than to marry a French Comte. They duly visited together the sights of London (such as Hyde Park and the Crystal Palace) but one night at Covent Garden – they were in a box for *Don Giovanni* – Villiers became extremely voluble, some say incoherent. One witness refers to his 'tumultuous lyricism' but Laforgue's friend Gustave Kahn says it was a discourse on Hegel. The girl is said to have been terrified but it is also possible that, as a music-lover, she simply wanted to hear the Mozart. Whatever the reason, she came to her senses and fled – later to be immortalized *malgré elle* as Alicia Clary in Villiers' *L'Eve future*. But in the meantime, while waiting to write that masterpiece, Villiers was obliged to seek his return ticket from the Consulate.

Well, that was that. I was preparing to gather up my books and return them to the island in the centre of the Reading Room when I got the word that an alarm was in progress . . .

This is a contemporary fact of life at the BM. All the doors have to be shut, so that the people outside the museum can't get in (they stand around kicking their heels) and the people inside can't get out (they miss their various appointments, such as the dentist or a Mozart opera matinee). Nobody knows the reasons for these alarms, but it is all taken seriously and the implication is that there has been skulduggery. Some say that Melina Mercouri has been spotted near the Elgin Marbles. Others think the alarm was set off accidentally by schoolboys barging into show-cases. Nobody mentions terrorists and bombs because that might bring bad luck. Whatever it is, it's usually a nuisance.

On this occasion it turned out to be a bonus, for it made me sit down again and turn to a book of Villiers letters, where almost immediately I found one to Mallarmé dated January 1874. It was ecstatic and I wondered if it had been written very early in the idyll or whether Villiers was just whistling in the dark. It began 'Dearling [sic] Stéphane' and went on to say that everything was wonderful and that if

Stéphane could see him now he would surely exclaim: 'Aoh! That is the most elegant and lovely gentleman I never knew. Is it possible that it was the poor fellow called Villiers? Aoh! very strange! very curious indeed . . .'

Dropping back exhausted into his native French, he says that he is in love with an angel – 'the positively last, my dear chap, and after this they can pull away Jacob's ladder. I'm in love with my only possible wife. Her millions? Well yes, there is that too. It's natural for a star to give off rays but never forget that she's still a heavenly body in her own right. All day long she calls me her own, her very own Auguste.' (And Auguste calls her 'R' because the letter 'R' is pronounced Eyre in French.) He only mentions two contretemps: she is under age and her father has promised her to someone else, but why worry? 'We'll just wait for a dark night and then I'll carry her off in the fog.'

In his reply Mallarmé compliments Villiers on his excellent English and there is the dreadful possibility that he really meant it, since Villiers' English is no worse than Mallarmé's own.

But a voice now comes on the Reading Room tannoy, apologizing for the inconvenience and announcing that the doors are now open. Melina has been apprehended or the schoolboys ejected. I still don't know why the Comte de La Houssaye allowed the Comte de Villiers to keep his teeth. Was there a struggle? It is disturbing to think of two Comtes fighting. Was anyone actually bitten? It is one of those things you never find out, even at the British Library.

Villiers de L'Isle Adam

67 Charlotte St

When the Commune Came to Fitzrovia

hough grateful to England for the sanctuary it offered, the French Communards found London a problem. Typical in his feelings of love-hate was the writer-revolutionary Jules Vallès, whose bestseller *Londres dans la rue*, very strong on hate, should be read in tandem with his letters, where other sentiments come through.

'London is lugubrious,' he says. 'The rain is black and the inhabitants are a gloomy lot. Away from the busy streets there's a terrible sadness; and the busy streets themselves are an avalanche of crowds and noise, like a rabble army in retreat. But there's also a grandeur about it all, and that feeling of freedom to do what one wants, to be poor or to be rich. I'd rather live in London than Geneva, Lausanne, The Hague, Brussels, Nantes or Rouen. A stroll round London really shakes you up: even Paris will seem tame after this.'

To a fellow Communard who has chosen Lugano and isn't too happy, he says: 'Plunge into a great city: you rust more surely in sunshine than in fog. More sick men would survive if, from their beds, they could see the street. So come to London. I absolutely recommend this black town. London, the immense London, with the British Museum in the middle of it.'

The British Museum he describes variously as 'a huge and unimaginable bonus' and 'a town in itself, full of riches with benign administrators'. They are serious and efficient, he says, but they all wear roses or carnations in their button-holes. 'I'm writing from there now. Two yards away sits Regnard, with Lissagaray next to him. Pilotelle's just passed and Pyat is due any moment. It's a whole world. Everything and everyone's here. We meet between the rows of desks like people in a village street.'

But outside the Museum things were less cosy. The French Government kept tabs on the refugees, thanks to the sinister detective Houillier and his army of informers. Here, for instance, is a typical report on Vallès from the Paris police archives (Ba. 879: item 468): 'London, 17 Nov 1878. – Have followed the man Vallès for these past two days. On Friday morning he walked to the British Museum, returning home at 3 p.m. He emerged again at six and made his way to Mme Audinet's restaurant, where he dined. At 8.30 he left the restaurant for Veglio's café and there played dominoes with the Corsican Cialdini, an inferior water-colour painter (non-political). Vallès was home by 12.30. Yesterday (Saturday) he did the same.'

One day Vallès offers advice to his Lugano friend in case he should still come to London. The trick for survival, he says, is to live equidistant from the British Museum and a large park (Hyde or Regent's). This was the recipe for a healthy life and, in the case of the Communards, the clear answer was Fitzrovia, though the district had not yet acquired that name. If they chose to settle north of Oxford Street, it was perhaps to distance themselves from the common run of French residents and tourists who tended to mill around Soho and Leicester Square. The Communards were inclined to spurn these people, whom they regarded as little better than petty criminals.

The main street of their own village was the beloved Charlotte Street, and their town hall was the wine and food store of Victor Richard, a three-storey house numbered 67. Still a wine shop today, it stands opposite the headquarters of Channel 4. As for the splendid Victor Richard, he was a cheerful Burgundian who introduced the coffee-mill to England and with it the art of coffee-making in the French manner. A lively entrepreneur, he made a substantial income and gave much of it away to his fellow Communards whom he fed almost single-handed. Well able to cope with the dreaded Inspector Houillier, he also served them as watch-dog. A few houses along the street, at number 59, was the excellent restaurant of Mme Elisabeth Audinet, where the spy had followed Vallès; and Veglio's café, scene of the domino game, was round the corner at 17 Tottenham Court Road. It was a tight-knit and fairly safe community: Victor had trained his assistant René to recognize a police spy at fifty paces.

Vallès himself lived two hundred yards away, opposite the Middlesex Hospital, at 38 Berners Street. His attic room, too hot in the summers of 1875-9, was just as draughty in winter. But it was here that he wrote the first book (*L'Enfant*) of his trilogy *Jacques Vingtras*. Though he never had much money, there was always someone in those days poorer than oneself. And so it was that he acquired a devoted slave called Vincent Oldfield, on whom he relied to perform every sort of odd job as well as routine translating and copying. In Oldfield Vallès must have realized that he had discovered a Dickensian character *en chair et en os*. At one point in the letters Vallès has fled to Greenwich to escape his creditors. 'I am writing to you in the topmost room of an inn,' he tells his friend. 'I am facing the Observatory, the silly park and the stupid deer. Am completely disorientated and without even a change of shirt because I haven't seen the wretched Oldfield for four days.'

By 1880, however, an amnesty had allowed Vallès to return to the Continent, where he met the beautiful and talented 'Séverine', a girl less than half his age whom he trained to become one of the great journalists of her day. In order to put the finishing touches to *Londres dans la rue* he returned to London in the summer of 1883, staying inevitably chez Victor at 67 Charlotte Street, where he found the high-ceilinged *piano nobile* room pleasantly cool. The letters he wrote home provide an exacting course in journalism for poor Séverine, who is put through her paces like a young apprentice. The postscripts are terse but eloquent: 'Am just off on a round of the pubs, where I'll certainly see some horrors . . . I survived those pubs. Now for Wapping . . . Tonight it's Whitechapel, more bestiality . . .'

Yet afterwards he tended to forget the horrors of London and remember only those gentlemen-librarians of the British Museum Reading Room, with their flowery button-holes. 'They believed in God and the Queen,' said Vallès 'and they served every reader equally, no matter how he was dressed.'

Tissot

The End of an Anglophile

James Tissot grew up in the shipyard town of Nantes, and later gravitated to Paris to become a famous painter. But in May 1871 he found himself – like many Frenchmen after the Commune – in London. He was 35.

That same year Kathleen Newton, an Irish girl who had fled from an arranged marriage in India, had arrived back in England divorced, pregnant and tubercular. She was 17.

Tissot had always been in love with England; in fact he had changed his name from Jacques-Joseph to James to underline the fact. A fellow painter, Jacques-Emile Blanche, was convinced at a first meeting that he was indeed an Englishman. And as an intimate friend of Thomas Gibson Bowles, founder of *Vanity Fair* magazine, Tissot had everything going for him in England: he would set the Thames on fire and make it his own. As a native of Nantes he knew all about boats and Whistler had shown the way: in no time at all Tissot was commuting between Gravesend and Greenwich and answering to the unlikely title of the 'Watteau of Wapping'.

Such was his success that by 1873 he had bought a fairytale house in St John's Wood, with an enormous garden and (according to Edmond de Goncourt) 'a manservant in silk stockings to brush and polish the leaves.'

To suggest the ambiance of Late Victorian St John's Wood, Nikolaus Pevsner in *The Buildings of England* quotes Elizabeth Bowen and her phrase 'a faint impropriety'. He applies it to the very corner of Grove End Road (at the Abbey Road junction) where Tissot came to live. The house featured a garden pool which Tissot greatly enlarged, building around it a colonnade copied from the Parc Monceau in Paris. Inside the house he installed a replica of the famous bay window of the Trafalgar Inn, Greenwich, where he had eaten many a whitebait supper.

In the meantime the much put-upon Kathleen Newton had been sent to live with her sister Mary Hervey in Hill Road, which was just around the corner from Tissot. By now she had a daughter, and would soon have a son by Tissot himself: by 1876 the famous painter and the disgraced Irish girl were living together in the big house at 44 Grove End Road.

The liaison lasted six years and in the early days was idyllically happy. But a public outcry soon developed and the couple were ostracized by society, having to withdraw more and more completely into the house and garden of No. 44. Since most of his pictures now featured Kathleen, James Tissot was accused in print of 'flaunting his domestic arrangements at the Grosvenor Gallery' (a reference to the fine new artists' showcase in Bond Street). For six years Kathleen Newton, her health now failing, was obliged to live as a recluse in the vast garden Tissot had made for her: only there was she free from prying eyes and prattling tongues. And while she began the long process of dying there was a sad feeling of charade, if not theatre, in Tissot's string of pictures depicting her as the happy bride and mother, surrounded by husband, children and friends. The colonnade, pool and Trafalgar window began to seem like props, reminiscent of Anouilh's play *Léocadia* where similar props became part of the protagonists' sentimental life. Even Willingham, the white-haired old gardener, was pressed into service as a model, all in the cause of representing the happy domestic life.

Kathleen died on 9 November 1882, aged 28, and was buried at Kensal Green. Five days later (14 November) Tissot was back in Paris. He had left the house exactly as it was . . . his paint-brushes where they happened to be lying. The break was complete: England had made his name and also destroyed him.

Willingham stayed on in his little lodge, and was seen by the neighbours burning Kathleen's mattress and other belongings in the garden. Eventually Tissot sold the place to a famous colleague, Sir Lawrence Alma-Tadema, who added sundry Greco-Roman features, as well as scattering his initials (AT) at every corner of the property as if to establish territorial rights.

The house today looks pleasantly dilapidated. Five minutes

from St John's Wood tube station, it is let off in flats, no longer under siege, with the garden gate flung wide open. On the site of the colonnaded pool a row of lock-up garages now stands, but some of Tissot's chestnut trees survive in the much reduced garden. And a rather splendid ilex tree, which he must also have known, droops over the front wall and on to the pavement of Grove End Road.

Jacques-Emile Blanche thought Kathleen a typical beauty of her day, in the style of Lily Langtry. Edmond de Goncourt called her 'la Mauperin anglaise' after one of his own heroines.

One of Tissot's biographers, Christopher Wood, drew attention to the 'distinct note of moral disapproval spiced with envy' which hounded Tissot and Kathleen at St John's Wood. The same feelings were strikingly in evidence on the occasion of Tissot's Barbican show a hundred years later.

44 Grove End Road
St. John's Wood

A Job in the City

The critic I. A. Richards once recalled visiting T. S. Eliot at the Lloyds Bank Colonial and Foreign Department in King William Street. Some time in the late 1970s I made a little investigation of my own. I found that Stafford House, 20 King William Street, though no longer part of the Lloyds empire, remained very much as it was when Eliot began work there on 17 March 1917. It was not difficult to discover the row of basement rooms, described by Richards as extremely small, with the glass squares of the pavement only a few feet from Eliot's head as he worked. Knowing the interest and pride that Lloyds have always taken in their distinguished ex-employee, I approached the Bank Archivist, Mr M. D. Roberts, with the proposal that he positively identify which of the rooms was Eliot's and set up a plaque. Mr Roberts promised to consider the idea but in the early 1980s he wrote to say that Stafford House was now empty and the subject of a demolition application. The eight-storey office building to be erected on this corner site by London Bridge should have been called Eliot House. Our hopes were dashed. Phoenix House is the name they gave it.

However, Eliot was not the only poet to work in the City. His own office may have vanished but there is still time to put a plaque on 15 St Swithin's Lane, where Paul Valéry worked for a time.

It was on 30 March 1896 that Valéry left Paris for London on a mysterious mission. Describing it thirty years later in English decidedly better than Mallarmé's he said: 'I was then leading a strange life.' (He was 24 years old but had already written *La Soirée avec Monsieur Teste*.) 'I lived waiting for I do not know what incident to turn up and change my life. My trunk was always at the foot of my bed as a symbol of the departure I was ready to take upon the slightest token by Fate. I held myself in readiness to obey any call or external intervention giving me the signal to transform this stagnant life. I was therefore ready to go when, about the beginning of '96, I received a letter from London. A post, about which no particulars were given, was offered me there in a letter signed with an unknown name. I had to decide at once, wire my reply the same day . . .'

At 9 a.m. on Tuesday 31 March he arrived at Victoria. A cab conveyed him to 12 Burleigh Mansions, Charing Cross Road. There he met a man who worked for Cecil Rhodes (and perhaps also for French Intelligence). 'By eleven,' he told his friend André Gide, 'I was already at my desk in the City.'

The British South Africa Company, which had received its royal charter some seven years earlier, was just then in need of the most sensitive Press coverage. As Valéry puts it, 'It was the time of the Jameson Raid. The Chartered Company had rather extensive Press departments and my duty was to watch over relations with the Press in France.'

Although the house in St Swithin's Lane is today occupied by a bank, it retains in the foyer the miniature but ornate staircase, bearing an intricate monogram and the date 1888, which Valéry must have climbed daily on the way to his small office. To Gide on Thursday 2 April he writes that, although he's been only two days in London, the maddest things are happening:

'I'm caught in a mesh involving infinitely powerful men. Through my job, which is one of trust, I have learnt extremely important things. I handle the most revealing documents and beg you never to speak of what I am telling you here. My eyes were opened on Tuesday last to certain aspects of a mighty enterprise called the Chartered Company, which is in the process of acquiring the whole of South Africa. An extraordinary affair. The general public knew nothing of it until the Jameson Raid and the Transvaal business. You simply have no idea of the power and depth and wisdom and brutal clarity of these men . . .'

Valéry at a later date spoke of the sort of people he saw at St Swithin's Lane which he described as 'an unparalleled collection of the most diverse types of humanity, a humanity of adventurers. Occasionally could be seen strange wrecks, men to whom no other perspective was left than suicide.' There is a touch of *Heart of Darkness* here, a hint of those horrors to which Eliot himself was no stranger, though Valéry at the moment seems more fascinated by them than afraid.

In the letter to Gide he reported that he had taken a room in the Bloomsbury apartment house of Mrs Elizabeth Jane Rowell at 15 Grenville Street, but he didn't like it much: he found it lonely and the food disgusting, so he spent much of his leisure time tramping round the City and along the riverside. He even wrote a prose poem inspired by the same passage in Dante that later suggested Eliot's own lines:

> *A crowd flowed over London Bridge, so many,*
> *I had not thought death had undone so many.*

In Valéry's version he is crossing the bridge and stops to contemplate the view that he loves. Transfixed by sheer delight, he nonetheless senses at his back a blind and invisible army streaming endlessly past, drawn by its own pressing needs. As the great flow, impelled to fill a sort of vacuum, moves ever onwards he tries to ignore the dead, hurrying footsteps. And he catches the bitter taste of indefinable guilt, for has he not cut himself off from his fellow men in denying them life? 'On London Bridge,' he says, 'I found myself guilty of the crime of poetry.'

Why did he finally leave London? Did the work just dry up, or did his powerful employers decide that he was too intelligent a Frenchman to be let loose indefinitely among the secrets of the Chartered Company? Valéry's own explanation (written especially for the *Bookman's Journal* of December 1925) is not altogether convincing: 'I spent a few weeks in those offices, but now the London climate was the weather of February [actually it was April], the season when the fogs did not fail to try my southern constitution. Before long I had to give up the Chartered Company in England. Had it not been for influenza, I might have stayed. I had got accustomed to English life, and as I had no literary ambition, I could well have settled there, where I found my substance and livelihood.'

London Bridge

Zola and the Lost Hairpins

n the winter of 1898 the nursemaids of Upper Norwood became conscious of being watched a little too closely by a bearded gentleman wearing pince-nez and a bowler hat. Little did they know that the bowler was a cunning disguise: they were being subjected to the acute gaze of the leading exponent of literary realism. And the reason for his deep interest in the nannies was purely professional: he was gathering notes for his new novel *Fécondité*, later to be translated by his English friend E. A. Vizetelly as *Fruitfulness*.

Earlier that year Zola had made his stand in support of Dreyfus, culminating in the famous 'J'Accuse' letter in the newspaper *L'Aurore*. Convicted of libelling the General Staff, he had been sentenced to a year's imprisonment but had escaped to England, where he arrived on 19 July. From the Grosvenor Hotel, Victoria, he sent urgent word to the faithful Vizetelly, who spirited him away, first to Wimbledon and then to the Thames Valley. Three happy months he spent cycling around Walton, Weybridge and Addlestone, his only disguise the bowler but changing his surname every other week.

As winter approached a more permanent residence was needed and this was found at the Queen's Hotel, Church Road, Crystal Palace, a popular haven for distinguished foreign guests travelling incognito. Situated on high ground away from the winter fogs it was also (and still is) a noted venue for South Bank wedding breakfasts. This suited Zola well enough: from wedding breakfasts to fruitfulness being but a step.

Zola's stay in England was written up by Vizetelly in the *Evening News*. Serious consideration is given to the English birthrate and the rearing of English children. Zola was all for breast-feeding: he was sad to note that in this respect English-women had embarked on the same downward path as their French sisters. Indeed the ladies of Upper Norwood seemed hardly to see their children at all. They spent their days visiting and receiving, playing lawn-tennis or bicycling, handing over all their responsibilities to nursemaids.

'He often watched the troupes of children and nurse-maids,' said Vizetelly, 'during his afternoon strolls to Beulah Spa. He told me how they neglected their charges and stood about, endlessly flirting and gossiping.' And just to prove that he had not forgotten how to observe scientifically, the old master of *naturalisme* told Vizetelly that he often amused himself by counting the number of hairpins left lying on the pavement.

'Then he proceeded to ocular demonstration,' says Vizetelly. 'As we walked on for an hour or so we counted all the hairpins we could see. There were about four dozen. And he was careful to point out that we had chiefly followed a route where there was but a moderate amount of perambulator traffic. Not one man in a thousand would have thought of counting the lost hairpins and, if I tell this anecdote which some may think puerile, it is by way of illustrating my friend's powers of observation.'

If Zola, in the case of the lost hairpins, seems to emulate Sherlock Holmes, Vizetelly certainly played up to him as Dr Watson. 'On one point I told him he was surely wrong: if the

women lost their hairpins it must partly be because they had bought cheap ones with insufficient 'twists'. The cheap hairpins never caught properly in their coiled-up tresses. The women tossed their heads perchance and the hairpins fell to the ground. Supposing one hundred women passed along a certain street in the course of a day, it would not be surprising to find at least thirty hairpins lost there. And I concluded that, to the best of my belief, the cheap hairpins were made in Germany.'

This apparently left Zola speechless, but the two friends continued to discuss the mating habits of Upper Norwood. 'At Christmas I told him of the privilege that attached to mistletoe in England, so he bought himself a huge branch which he placed over the mantelpiece, even though there were no young ladies to kiss.'

That was the story as told to the readers of the *Evening News*. They were not permitted to know that Zola was visited in England by his mistress Jeanne Rozerot and the two children she had given him. It was all the inspiration he needed to finish *Fécondité* before leaving the Queen's Hotel for France on 4 June 1899.

Queen's Hotel

Zola

The Incident at Box Hill

lphonse Daudet came to England to see George Meredith, and the meeting duly took place at Box Hill in May 1895 – but their parting on the railway station afterwards was even more memorable.

Daudet leaned out of the carriage to embrace his host who – not to be outdone – threw his trembling arms round the Frenchman in sudden abandon.

But the train had begun to move, and the two European celebrities could not disentangle themselves. They were now truly inseparable.

Meredith was carried off down the platform, unable to unclasp Daudet, who in turn could not shake off the Grand Old Man of English Letters.

How would it all end? Their carriage had reached the ballast at the end of the platform when a resourceful young guard stopped the train, and the reluctant traveller was lowered gently to the ground.

Meredith survived but Daudet never returned.

Annie. Annie made an excuse and left. Quarrels broke out once more, and late one night the Playden family feared he would break down the door of No. 75.

But after Kostro had returned to Paris a subtle change seems to have come over Annie. To show there was no ill-will she sent him a New Year card. So did her 15-year-old sister Jenny. Then Jenny sent him a photograph of Annie 'which Annie had thrown away', asking him to keep it a secret. Professor Michel Décaudin (who revealed these letters in the *Revue des Lettres Modernes*, No. 183-8) thinks that the little sister was put up to it by Annie herself. Early in April Annie asks bluntly (and it would be churlish to correct her French): 'Quand viendrez vous me voir! Je serai gentille!! cherie Ne plus méchant; *peut-être* – Annie.' Kostro must have urged her to come to Paris instead because on 23 April she writes him a full-blown letter in English:

75 Landor Road

75 Landor Road
London SW

Dear Kostro,

What you ask is impossible! I could not think of coming to you like that. No! – I want *you* to come to *London* as you promised! You have not seen me for six months and possibly your love for me will change.

I do *not* detest you as much as I used to, & if I were sure you would be true and faithful to me *always*, I might try to love you, Kostro. But I will promise *nothing* unless I see you. I have much to tell you and to ask you. So *if you love me* come to see me the first week in Mai (sic), as you have promised.

Otherwise I shall go away and you will, perhaps, never see me again.

Now *will* you *come* or *not*.
J'attends ta lettre.
Ta gentille chérie
                    X
               Annie

So, encouraged by the X no doubt, Guillaume came to London a second time and on 5 May we find Annie writing to him c/o Konitza (who in the meantime has married his weepy girlfriend and set up house in Chingford). Once again we give Annie's French as it comes:

75 Landor Road
midnuit

Chéri,

Je trouve que ma mère est vraiment malade et il faut absolument que je arrest chez moi demain. Si tu achète tes chaussures à Londres demain cherie Tu peux venir chez moi dans le après-midi Veux tu? fait mes excuses à Madame et Monsieur Konitza Mille baisers cherie Ton Annie.

And on 26 May, after he has returned to Paris, there is this final card in fractured French, which Apollinaire kept carefully with all the others till the day he died:

Merci pour carte chère Je pense à toi N'oublier pas ton photographie pour moi Mille baiser Penser à moi Annie Bonjour à ta mère.

What had happened in London? On 30 June Apollinaire wrote to a friend, saying that he had spent an exquisite month there, during which he had seen some divine Englishwomen, including one more beautiful than the rest.

But it was also at this moment that Annie decided that a job in America offered more to her than Kostro in Paris. It was a fateful decision for them both.

Still in a state of shock Apollinaire took up again a poem he had begun writing some months earlier: 'La Chanson du Mal-Aimé' ('Song of the Ill-Loved'). After an almost tender opening line: 'Un soir de demi-brume à Londres' ('On an evening of light mist in London') the Chanson proceeds savagely, leaving no doubt that he felt betrayed and was seeing the streets of London through the eyes of a man half crazed. It is an almost Baudelairean vision of a great city by someone who feels alienated from it, as though trapped at the bottom of the sea. Throughout the poem terror alternates with tenderness as he remembers desperately 'the girl I lost last year in Germany'. It is a theme he will return to in 'L'Emigrant de Landor Road' and in the quieter 'Annie', where he imagines her walking alone in a rose-garden on the Gulf of Mexico. Annie, in America, did receive a card from him, bearing Oscar Wilde's words: 'Yet each man kills the thing he loves.' To her the words suggested not regret but menace, and she instructed her parents to forward nothing more.

Much later (in 1915) he admitted to a friend that many of the expressions in the Chanson had been 'too severe and insulting towards a girl who understood nothing about me and who loved me in her way, but was disconcerted to find herself loving that strange creature, a poet. I loved her physically but our minds were poles apart. And yet she was subtle and gay. I was jealous without reason and her absence only exaggerated the pain. But my poem does suggest fairly well the way I felt . . . Twice I went to see her in London, but marriage was impossible and when she went to America that was that. Yet to see how much I suffered you have only to read that poem, in which I thought myself unloved, though really it was I who didn't love enough'.

Apollinaire died two days after the Armistice of 1918. Though Spanish flu was the immediate cause, resistance had been weakened by the war wound for which he underwent trepanation. This fact was recognized by the French Government who, because he 'died for France', extended his copyright period accordingly.

The story does not end there. Years later (after the Second World War) Annie was discovered to be alive and well, not on the Gulf of Mexico, but in Santa Barbara, California. To Dr Robert Goffin, the Belgian writer who traced her there, she expressed bewilderment and disbelief: she had never known that Kostro was famous or even that he was a poet – she had never heard the name Apollinaire. The following extracts from her correspondence with Dr Goffin are printed here for the first time in the original English by courtesy of Mme Simone Huysmans, Curator of the Apollinaire Museum at Stavelot, Belgium:

He predicted that something wonderful would happen to me before I died. I think [this news] coming to me through you is wonderful. It's unbelievably strange to have Guillaume brought back into my life in this way after 45 years . . . He was right in saying that I did not understand so strange a poet. I was too young and innocent. He frightened me at times. Did you know him personally? I think perhaps I knew a different Guillaume from the one you know as a poet. I knew him at 20. He was madly in love. I was a little fool. I could not allow myself to love him, partly on account of my puritanical upbringing, and then the Comtesse de Milhau filled my young head with stories of the deceit of men . . . He was at times impetuous and forceful to the point of cruelty, but could also be most considerate and loving. He was selfish of my company and also insanely jealous. The language was a barrier to better understanding . . . Yet there were times when we understood each other. I think the strength of his love was hypnotic to my innocence and simplicity. However, our romance ended tragically for me: I left my parents' home and came to America to forget and start a new life. Guillaume tried to find me but without success. Those who love his poetry should be grateful to me for not marrying him. Had I done so, such poetry might never have been written.

In the course of this long letter (dated 28 August 1946) Annie twice makes the point that 'the real story of our romance cannot be written – I'm sure Guillaume would not wish it . . . My memory brings back some incidents of that time, which I'm sure he would not write about.' As 'English Annie' she thanks Dr Goffin for bringing her 'the realization of Guillaume's love' and only regrets that it is too late now for her to apologize to Kostro himself 'for my lack of under-standing'. She still has an amethyst he gave her, which he said was 'part of a necklace belonging to a princess'. A splendid Apollinairean touch!

In another letter (12 November 1946) Annie speaks of the first and last times she ever saw him:

I remember the day he came for the interview. He smiled at me as he was leaving . . . Later he told me that his friends asked if the Countess was lovely, and he replied 'No, but the governess is!' . . . We had some beautiful walks at Honnef, beautiful and unforgetta-ble. Up snow-covered mountains. One in particular I have never forgotten: I would not be surprised if Guillaume has written about it. It was most beautiful and he was in a gentle mood that day, Gabrielle was with us . . . I remember going to the [London] station to see him off on his return to Paris. I shall never forget the expression on his face as he leaned out of the train window to look at me . . . He had the same expression when he left Neuglück, his eyes were dark and like velvet . . . He would have done anything I wished, but I would have nothing. I was, without doubt, a very foolish young woman.

As an ironic footnote the one lady who did recognize Kostro as a poet was Anna von Fisenne of Krayerhof, as Marc Poupon revealed in the *Revue des Lettres Modernes* (Nos.183-8). After giving him a place to work and making sure he was on the trip round Germany, she followed his subsequent career with keen interest. And, looking down on her when she died, was a painting she had acquired of Apollinaire after his trepanation, wearing the famous head bandage.

Annie became in her declining years a favourite with Apollinaire's American admirers. Interviewed in 1951 and 1962 by LeRoy Breunig and Francis Steegmuller, she still remained enigmatic as to her exact relations with the poet, just as she twice promised Dr Goffin she would do. When she was 82 Steegmuller described her as 'the most delightful-looking person imaginable: plump, white-haired, rosy-cheeked . . . and her eyes were a gay cornflower blue, far brighter than the blue blossoms printed on the dress she was wearing. Here truly was the Bluebird sung by Apollinaire in "La Tzigane".'

At 85 she was fêted at Barnard College, New York, and a photograph shows how much at ease she was made to feel. With Professor Breunig she was indeed always willing to answer 'picayunish' questions about her early life and would even talk about her so-called 'wicked' eyes, which the Coun-tess had apparently called 'hawk eyes'. But she still kept her secrets, as well as Kostro's.

Annie died on 29 December 1967, four weeks short of her 88th birthday and 50 years after the poet she had inspired and rejected.

The Strange Fête at Gunnersbury

ne of the prototypes of Alain-Fournier's enchanted château in *Le Grand Meaulnes* may have been a Congregational church in West London.

The young Frenchman (he was 18) had come to England in 1905 to improve his English. For two or three months he was to work in the Sanderson factory off Turnham Green, while staying with the company secretary, Mr J. J. Nightingale, at 5 Brandenburg (now Burlington) Road.

England had always been for him the land of adventure (of Defoe and Stevenson). Immediately he was thrilled by the country views in the train from Newhaven: 'the fields and trees all so green.' Chiswick was magical: 'My little room is on the second floor of a villa lost in greenery. Vaguely downstairs I hear the lawn being watered, and vaguely I hear Missiz Nightingale playing the piano, as all Englishwomen do. From time to time a train whistles on the way to Richmond . . . The suburban streets resemble country roads which are lined with châteaux of Sologne touching one another . . . When an Englishman smells a lime tree, he stops immediately, takes a deep breath and exclaims, "Oh, lovely!".'

Some of the glamour that Fournier found in Chiswick is still there. Re-tracing his walks one can still come across sylvan glades like Stavely Road holding out against the traffic of Hogarth Roundabout. One of the picture postcards he sent home was of 'Grove Park': to come upon that little scene today, where so little has changed – where the Grove Park pub and the letter-box are precisely where he left them – is strangely moving.

Fournier was also fascinated by English women. 'But I can't get used to them, it's partly the way they dress, which is too comfortably and too briefly and the colours too light. It took me a long time to figure out what puzzles me most about them, and then I realized that not one wears a corset, which gives them a loose, floppy look. That and the eternal bicycle and a boyish nose-in-the-air stance.'

In a long letter dated 23 July 1905 to his friend Jacques Rivière in Paris he devoted a whole section to what he called The Feminine Sex, which he found vastly different in England from what it was in France:

'Let me tell you about one small adventure with one small English girl: it's sweetly amusing and nothing more . . . In the room where I work – for about ten minutes every hour – I have facing me (across a wide desk littered with dictionaries, huge ledgers and typewriters) three girls. And behind me, on the other side of a glass partition, there's an army of clerks doing sums . . . Two of the girls are splendid creatures with remarkable figures, who spend the whole time looking for a chance to flirt. They are certainly fine girls but not my type, and I don't want to get involved with them and the clerks, so (despite constant peals of laughter) I maintain a stony silence and that otherwise occupied look of a gentleman whose thoughts are far, far away.

But the third girl happens to be the one that was first detailed to show me around and whom I at once summed up as: nice eyes and no body (it just doesn't exist), nineteen but looks twenty-three, with funny little face . . . I noticed too that, though shy and reserved, she made great efforts to be amiable . . . So one night about six, when she was struggling to get her tiny arms round the big ledgers, I gallantly jumped up and in a twinkling bundled everything into the safe – for which I received a thank-you, a smile and a blush.

Well, a couple of days ago, I noticed that Miss Nightingale took to school sundry pots of flowers. They were having a flower-show, like everyone else in London at the moment. There was to be a garden-party all afternoon and evening, at which the little girls were to sell ices. Clara invited me to come and buy one from her, but jokingly I asked her the price and told her it was too much, whereupon Mr N., pretending to be me, announced: 'Afraid I have to be elsewhere, Miss.'

After tea, about seven, I'd completely forgotten about Miss N. and had no intention of going to her fête. Instead, I went out to post a letter. I knew vaguely that her school was connected with a church, and that the whole thing more or less happened in church, but I had no idea where it was. However, on my way to the letter-box, I saw this little path leading to a sort of church, which was illuminated. A programme was posted up outside, which I stopped to read because these days I'm always glad to learn new words. I had just got to a bit about 'strolling at leisure in the illuminated garden' when Mr and Mrs N. strolled up themselves. Mr N. had a word with me and I was just moving on to the post when Mrs N. begged me to stay and see her daughter receive a prize.

I went into the little garden and at first saw only the bushes hung with fairy-lights. Then I noticed banks of flowers ranged along the walls of the bizarre little church, whose stained-glass windows were glowing dimly. Groups of young people came into my vision, and I noticed they included the dashing girls from the office. Farther on was a group of quieter, more serious girls. One of them detached herself. She was got up in a strange little Directoire hat. After first nodding to the N. family she held her hand straight out to me: it was my office friend. So there we were, the two of us, making heroic efforts to understand each other – and, to my own surprise, succeeding.

It was clear that she had made a big effort to come and speak to me, and the English words I heard her say have since fixed themselves on my mind with the special life they had that evening. I can still hear the way she said should *to denote obligation rather than the merely conditional: 'You should have come earlier.'*

The small-talk we exchanged concerned minuscule things, such as can only be discussed beneath a small Directoire hat with someone whose English is strictly limited. 'I go to this church every Sunday, that's why I'm here now. Tomorrow I go on holiday but ten days is too little, isn't it?' – 'But whatever shall I do without you?' – 'Oh really, for you the work isn't difficult, is it?' Like all English women she makes enormous use of the gentle 'is it?' and 'isn't it?' which turn the phrase into a question . . . I stayed there for almost an hour enjoying a special kind of pleasure which I described to myself, perhaps because of the church and hat, as 'methodist'. Then I left her with a shake of the hand and a phrase which I believe is exchanged formally between gentlemen but which seemed to express my feeling exactly: 'I am so happy to have met you.'

A couple of days later there was another garden-party, a much bigger affair, this time organized by Sanderson's themselves. Here again he met a girl wearing a small Directoire hat – it seems to have been the fashion in Chiswick that year. Actually it had nothing to do with Methodists: what he was observing was the tail-end of the Kate Greenaway style, which had so delighted his fellow-countryman Jules Laforgue some years earlier. The peaked bonnet with high crown and funnel back, tied with strings under the chin, was

still being worn by teenage girls in 1905. What is more important, both girls, with their distinctive hats, went straight into Fournier's novel, which he was even then preparing to write.

It is fair to say that more than just the hats went into his book. Much of the atmosphere of Clara's garden-party itself seems to be echoed in that section of the novel in which the children are staging 'La Fête Etrange' for the young master of the mysterious domain. And, as if in corroboration, the *Chiswick Times* of 21 July 1905 describes the fête at Gunnersbury Congregational Church the previous day as 'a flower-show in which the principal part was taken by the children.'

Did the music and the colour of a warm summer night in West London crystallize into the dream-like winter episode of 'La Fête Etrange'? As it happens, Fournier's church survived until quite recently (at 345a Chiswick High Road) but there was not much of magic there. Fifty yards back from the main road it stood abandoned, windows smashed, in a piece of rough wasteland. Now only the tarmac of a car-park marks the spot. Could it ever have had the glamour that Fournier's imagination gave to it?

'In England I drew from myself some rather touching poetry,' he wrote later. And it was from England that he sent home the strange self-portrait, showing him with a bandage round his head. In the event it was only a damp handkerchief to relieve a headache, but it gave him the idea of the romantic character Frantz de Galais who in *Le Grand Meaulnes* wears a similar bandage. At this time everything was grist to his mill. So why not Gunnersbury Congregational Church?

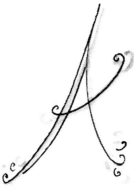

After the tragic death on 7 December 1893 of the child prostitute 'Monelle' (whom he had befriended two years earlier), the great French story-teller Marcel Schwob was so obviously shattered that his friends sought means to comfort him. One of them, Léon Daudet – whose fierce anti-Semitism did not deprive him of the luxury of an occasional Jewish friend – decided to bring him to England. The trip was a success: one convivial evening when they were strolling down the Strand together, arm in arm, they imagined they saw De Quincey and Dickens just ahead of them. The name De Quincey is probably the operative one here, for when they reached Charing Cross Station Schwob gave five

Schwob

golden louis (out of the ten in his pocket) to a girl who reminded him of Anne-of-Oxford-Street.

The gesture, which Daudet thought extravagant, was typical of Schwob. On the first page of *Le Livre de Monelle* he recalls an incident in the life of the young Napoleon: 'Bonaparte, the killer, was eighteen when he met, by the iron gates of the Palais-Royal, a little prostitute. She was pale and shivering but "one's got to live" she told him. No one knows the name of that girl whom Bonaparte took one November night to his room at the Hôtel de Cherbourg. She was from Nantes in Brittany, she was weak and tired and her lover had just left her. She was simple and good, and her voice had a sweet sound. I think that ever afterwards the sound of her voice moved Bonaparte to tears, and that he sought her a long time without finding her, in the winter evenings.'

Similarly Schwob remembered the voice of his *petite bête* Monelle when she used to say 'Je suis sage aujourd'hui' or 'Si j'étais un petit oiseau tu me mettrais dans ta poche, quand tu partirais'. For Schwob, indeed, was a collector of tiny birds, so small and fragile that in later years the only person allowed to play with them was his wife's friend Colette, an *amie des bêtes* if ever there was one.

Though he was childlike, Schwob was also the most erudite writer of his time. In his twenties, on that first trip to England, he dazzled Daudet with his knowledge of foreign languages, of writers past and present. Among contemporaries he liked Robert Louis Stevenson best of all: at the drop of a hat he would dress up as a pirate in his hero's honour. Even on that Channel crossing he was barred from the first-class restaurant for looking too much like a sea-dog out of *Treasure Island*. But he never met the author.

When he returned to London at the turn of the century, it was to be married; London marriages were fashionable among the French, they eliminated fuss. His friends were amazed that this far from handsome man had captured the young star of the Comédie-Française Marguerite Moreno, so admired for her intelligence and beauty by men like Valéry and Mallarmé. What captivated her, it seems, was the combination of limpid eyes, melodious voice and a generous soul.

The wedding took place at the City Registry Office, 61 Bartholomew Close, a building that still exists but only as a branch of Bart's Hospital. One of the witnesses was Stevenson's friend W. E. Henley and the couple booked in at the Cannon Street Hotel (where later the Smyrna merchant was to ask T. S. Eliot to luncheon 'in demotic French'). During the visit they saw Conan Doyle play cricket at Haslemere, an experience which left Schwob perplexed.

He was already ill, however, and the rest of his life was spent in a vain search for health, travelling in the steps of Stevenson. Usually he was accompanied by his Chinese servant Ting and his chihuahua Flip. The latter used to sit on his shoulder while he worked, but Ting was faithful too: he promised to follow his master to the ends of the earth on condition that his body be returned to China when he died. In the event it was Flip who died. Ting lived to be mocked by the inhabitants of Guernsey, an incident which greatly distressed Schwob.

Some previously unknown letters recently came to light in Paris, written by Schwob in English to the American Vincent O'Sullivan. They are very sad letters. In one of them he says: 'I go to Samoa as if to my final medicine'. He died in 1905 – not on Stevenson's island but on the Ile Saint-Louis in Paris, while his wife was away on tour, trying to earn a living for them both. In the 1920s she edited with great devotion the ten-volume edition of his works, and later crowned her own career with a legendary performance as Giradoux's *Mad Woman of Chaillot*.

Happy Housekeeping in Chelsea

As a friend of England (and of English women) Valery Larbaud deserves a place in a collection of 'Ententes Cordiales'. Like Louis Hémon he was that strange phenomenon, a Frenchman who preferred London to Paris.

He was in some ways a typical child of the age: a rich Edwardian with attributes which are labelled today as 'male chauvinist' – and yet he must have made many women happy. He sometimes tended to be an old-fashioned sentimentalist with his worship of little girls; but he also had an acute understanding of James Joyce, whose *Ulysses* he translated into French.

His understanding of English women was quite perceptive: he saw them as saint-devils flitting from prudery to abandon at the drop of a hat: a unique combination of hot and cold, both exaggerated, so that their demeanour when not in bed was as extreme as their passion when aroused. One of his achievements was to sensualize the category of 'intendante', a word that can mean anything from 'lady manager' to 'Mother Superior'. For Larbaud it meant a housekeeper who doubled as mistress.

The name that springs immediately to mind is 'Gladys', who appears several times in the relevant *Journal*, before and just after the First World War. Larbaud was a writer who was better at recording experience than imagining it, so that his life is often simply replayed as fiction. When he writes to his fellow poet Léon-Paul Fargue, from London in 1911, that he is finding life most enjoyable, living with a woman of modest means intellectually but who has a charming daughter as a bonus – he is giving a first sketch of the famous story he will write a few years later called 'Beauté, mon beau souci' (the title taken from Malherbe, it was first published in the *Nouvelle Revue Française*, July and August 1920).

The lady whose mental attainments leave something to be desired (Edith Crosland in the story) was either Gladys herself or someone who closely resembled her. She was (would have to be) a lively affectionate woman with a good sense of humour, whose life, perhaps as a widow, was no doubt leavened by Larbaud if only for a limited time (because, as an Edwardian, he was very conscious of the difference in class). The story makes clear that the lady welcomed this enterprising French male – but then of course it would.

Nothing is known of the charming daughter (Queenie in the story). In print at least she is a 14-year-old of the type that Larbaud found so desirable, platonically, when not embroiled with more mature women.

The quality shared by Edith Crosland and Gladys which most distressed Larbaud was not a lack of education but a pretension to it, something he identified as a touch of 'nordic pedantry'. 'Never mind philosophy,' he used to tell Edith. 'Just read the books you enjoy.'

The best thing in the story is its evocation of pre-war Chelsea. He describes lovingly how it has developed from a village, when it consisted of little more than Old Church Street, to its current perfection in 1911. Larbaud held the lease of his flat there for several years. As a rich man he could afford to winter abroad, but he always returned to London. There he observed life from the ground-floor window on the corner of Lordship Place and Lawrence Street, looking across to the Children's Centre where he first saw Queenie-Lolita arriving for a party in fancy-dress. The flat is still there – the one on the left as you go in – still waiting for a plaque to be put up. As a further hint to the Council the address is 1 Lawrence Mansions . . .

Valery Larbaud deserves better of the English. In some ways he is an historic figure, the first European, the man who wrote: 'This whole business of passports and consulates, of having to take seriously the matter of nationality, seems just silly to people like me, who never feel they belong to one particular country.'

If ever he had felt that, one can be certain the country would have been England, of which he wrote: 'Ah, tout de même, ce n'est pas amusant to quitter Londres et l'Angleterre.'

On another occasion he wrote: 'I could have spent a lot more time on Samuel Butler . . . but there was London and a London girl.'

When his *Journal* for the years 1912-1920 was published, nobody was surprised to find that, out of 75,000 words, 70,000 were written in English. Not long before he died he wrote (partly in French, mostly in English): 'Londres: the place in the world where I have been most happy.'

Poignant in a way (though treated by him as a great joke) was the time he called at the British Museum to correct a catalogue entry: they had spelt his first name 'Valérie' and he wished to apprise them of his gender.

Larbaud

A Frenchman in Stepney

During the twenties a book called *Maria Chapdelaine* established itself in France as one of the bestsellers of all time. Published posthumously, it was the work of Louis Hémon, who had died in 1913, aged 32. Apart from its commercial success it won a sure place in every history of French literature as the regional novel par excellence: it was the best book ever written about French Canada. In the wake of its success other MSS which the author had left with his sister Marie at Quimper began to emerge. All the rest of Louis Hémon's work was not about Canada but about London.

The life (and death) of Louis Hémon provides one of the lesser known curiosities of French literature, of particular interest to the English. It is not every day that a Frenchman falls in love with England and decides to make his life here. Louis Hémon made that firm decision when he was 20, after spending the summer holidays of 1901 at Oxford. Quite calmly he threw away a ready-made career in France and resisted family protests with typical 'British' phlegm. To his father, a senior civil servant, he wrote nonchalantly: 'You seemed to be wishing on me a whole lot of horrible happenings, such as changing my character, becoming more mature, improving my moral tone and I don't know what other mad adventures . . .' With quiet obstinacy he turned down an assured future in the French Colonial Service, for which he had already learnt Indo-Chinese, and set about learning English instead. He succeeded so well that in later years, whether in England or France, he was continually being taken for an Englishman.

As soon as possible after his military service he left for England. That was in 1903, the year in which his father became Inspecteur Général de l'Instruction Publique and when his uncle Louis had already been 23 years MP for Quimper.

Like Gustave Doré before him Louis Hémon was instinctively drawn to the Dickensian aspect of London, its sordid but impressive squalor. Like another Frenchman, Gavarni, he seems to have taken lodgings in Stepney, which after all would be convenient enough for his work as a clerk in the City. He just missed meeting Henri-Pierre Roché, the author of *Jules et Jim*, who had been teaching French at Toynbee Hall the year before (an experience which he describes in *Deux Anglaises et le Continent*).

In those days before the First World War London contained many more Frenchmen than it does now. Soho, for instance, could still be called the French Quarter. But none of those Frenchmen was more at home than Louis Hémon. He delighted in his new-found independence, the freedom of being abroad, but he was also glad to leave a certain stuffiness behind him. He was one of the new generation of Frenchmen who loved sport, especially the way it was practised in England. All the years he was here he wrote regularly for Paris sporting sheets such as *Le Vélo* and *L'Auto*, spent hours on the river, ran cross-country and never missed a big fight at 'Wonderland', the boxing arena in Whitechapel Road.

Even more than sport he loved just mooching round the East End observing the variety of people, notably the Jews and the Irish. Though shocked by the poverty, he found life in Stepney exciting because primitive. Two of his heroes (in

1 Lawrence Mansion

Colin-Maillard and *Battling Malone, Pugiliste*) were simple, bewildered Irishmen at odds with the world. It was inevitable that Louis Hémon should acquire an Irish girlfriend, Lydia O'Kelly, whose fate was to be linked closely with his own.

His first long story was *Lizzie Blakeston*, which he sent to *Le Temps* in August 1907 and which to his surprise they used as a six-part serial in the week beginning 3 March 1908. A polished piece of work, it concerns a little girl who lived at 12 Faith Street, off the Mile End Road. This street, a casualty of the Second World War, was situated between the Trinity Green almshouses and Forester's Music Hall, the site being occupied today by a modern housing estate. Life gets the better of little Lizzie when her hopes and dreams of being a music-hall star come crashing down. She finishes in the river, which seemed to Hémon a likely enough ending, given the time and place. He had far less optimism than

Hémon

Dickens, and the Irish heroes of his next two books came to equally sticky ends. In *Colin-Maillard* Mike goes berserk, strangles a pub owner and is presumably for the gallows. Pat in *Battling Malone* is shot dead by an aristocratic lady who has first provoked him to fury. To Louis Hémon in pre-war Stepney, death seemed a dénouement not only convenient but logical.

In putting down his despair on paper Hémon must have been encouraged by Arthur Morrison and his *Tales of Mean Streets*, but he certainly knew his East End as well as anyone. It would be hard to rival, for instance, his 50-word description of Cable Street, beginning at the east end of that excessively long thoroughfare:

Up as far as Watney Street the women wear their hair in curlers; beyond that point elaborate hair-do's are the rule. It is a detail which, taken in conjunction with the names over the shop-fronts, indicates that you have passed from Erin into Israel.

But after two world wars Hémon's East End is barely recognizable. The two great Hawksmoor churches have survived: St George's, whose bells used to wake Mike; and St Anne's, which Lizzie slipped past on her way to the river. Parts of Brick Lane and Old Montague Street Hémon might recognize, together with that stretch of Whitechapel Road by the London Hospital on a Saturday night – and Petticoat Lane on a Sunday morning. Until fairly recently the home of glamorous Hannah Hydleman (37 Cable Street) was still miraculously surviving, but not any more. And one rarely sees a Frenchman in these parts today. Sartre used to say that the real London is situated east of the Tower, but few Frenchmen bother to test the truth of that statement (except perhaps over pints at the Prospect of Whitby on the night after Twickenham).

Louis Hémon himself eventually turned his interest from the East End to the West. We find him running on Ruislip Common and spending Sundays at Richmond. *Colin-Maillard* was sent to *Le Temps* from an Import-Export office at 16 Henrietta Street, Covent Garden. (It was praised but returned.) That was at the end of 1908. The next spring he's in Kilburn, where a daughter is born at 32 Mazenod Avenue, says the birth certificate, to Lydia O'Kelly.

The wider knowledge he was gaining of London was used in his next book *Monsieur Ripois et la Némésis*, the tale of a French philanderer. One of its principal scenes is set at Dollis Hill, on what was then a bare hillock, 250 yards from the Edgware Road. Here the lovers meet several times and look east across the Edgware Road and its trams to the sidings of the old Midland Railway, while to the north the Welsh Harp glitters in the sun.

But Fate caught up with Louis Hémon and supplied the sort of ending he chose for his novels. Lydia O'Kelly had a mental breakdown and was admitted to Hanwell. In despair Hémon left his daughter with a sister of Lydia's (but she was registered in his own name and later adopted by his own sister). On his 31st birthday (14 October 1911) he sailed to Canada from Liverpool. During the last six months of 1912 he worked on the land at Péribonka, on the north shore of Lake St John, 180 miles north of Quebec, and it was from his experiences there that he wrote *Maria Chapdelaine* in the early part of 1913.

At the end of June he finished the typing in Montreal and sent it off to *Le Temps* in Paris. They wrote at once accepting but their letter was returned to them in August marked 'Décédé'. Immediately after posting the packet Hémon had left Montreal for Ontario. His plan was to make his way west by following the tracks of the Canadian Pacific Railway, accompanied by an Australian friend Harold Jackson. Both men were killed instantly on 8 July 1913 by a train that surprised them on a bend of the track.

When *Maria Chapdelaine* was published in *Le Temps* the following year (1914) it caused no great stir but it was carefully noticed and remembered by Mme Ludovic Halévy. After the war in 1921, when her son Daniel started the famous Cahiers Verts series for Bernard Grasset, she urged him to re-publish *Maria Chapdelaine* as his first book. Its instant and enormous success became a legend in France and was followed, also in the Cahiers Verts, by *Lizzie Blakeston, Colin-Maillard* and *Battling Malone* in 1923, 1924 and 1925.

Monsieur Ripois had an odder fate. An English translation was published in 1925 (in London and New York) but the original French version had to wait till the mid-1930s. Even then *Monsieur Ripois* made no real impact in France till the 1950s when it was turned into a light comedy film in which Gérard Philipe made the hero a good deal more charming than he really was. Speaking of the book (and significantly not the film) Jean Renoir wrote: 'It's a masterpiece that has the flavour of Raymond Queneau at his very best: a tale of squalor told by a man with a great heart.'

St. George in the East

47

4 Leicester St (Poon's)

From Meanwell College to Guignol's Band

or a long time it was thought that Céline's excursions to England, in such books as *Mort à crédit* and *Guignol's Band*, were merely a product of his feverish imagination. This seemed to be borne out by the crazy topography and fanciful English that went with the mad goings-on. More recently it has been revealed that Céline not only knew England well but spoke the language far better than he let on.

He first came here as a schoolboy of 14, when he spent half a term at Mr W. W. Tonkin's University School, 5-6 New Road, Rochester. That was in late February 1909, and the solid brick and stone buildings still stand at the top of Nag's Head Lane. Facing them is the vast sweep of hill, from the summit of which Céline described the fine view he admired of the Medway and the Three Towns. Since my last visit they have become part of a luxury hotel and restaurant – the Dickens – where the food will certainly be more plentiful than in Céline's day. This was the main reason he asked to be removed after only one month: he rebelled against the paltry offerings and the basement dining-room in which they were served.

At the end of March he pretended to be recalled to Paris but instead made his way to a better school at Broadstairs:

Le Cavalier
Céline

Pierremont Hall, where he was entirely happy and stayed till the following November. The original of Betsy Trotwood had lived at Pierremont Hall, and while there he was taken to Ramsgate to see *HMS Dreadnought*, then the world's largest battleship. Yet, despite these attractions, it was the Rochester school that he chose to immortalize as 'Meanwell College'.

In *Mort à crédit* he arrives at Rochester on a Saturday night, when a tremendous fair seems to be in progress down by the river, with drunken sailors milling amongst the stalls and a Salvation Army band at the pier-head. This was probably just the normal ambiance of a local Saturday night, but the young Frenchman gets so involved that time slips away without his noticing it. Indeed, dawn is breaking when he finally climbs the hill, accompanied by Gwendoline, a girl who sells fritters and likes foreigners, and a troupe of 'nigger minstrels' who wash the blacking off their faces at a convenient fountain on the way up. No wonder that, as he hammers on the side-door in Nag's Head Lane, it is opened by a pyjama'd Mr Tonkin in some dismay. But the poor man's troubles are only just beginning: little does he know that he has Céline for a pupil.

It is not long before the whole school begins to disintegrate: as the boys leave one by one Mr Tonkin (or rather his fictional counterpart Mr Merrywin) faces bankruptcy and takes to the bottle; while his wife, the famous Nora Merrywin, drowns herself in the Medway after first seducing fourteen-year-old Céline in the deserted dorm. These events were of course imaginary and the University School itself continued to flourish in the most eminently respectable manner for another forty years or so.

Six years went by before Céline once more ventured across the Channel. It was now May 1915 and he had recently been the hero of a sensational exploit of the First World War, when he was seriously wounded while delivering a vital message on horseback in the face of enemy fire. Invalided out of the army, he was given a temporary desk job at the French Passport Office, 18 Bedford Square (facing the Consulate, then at number 51). With a colleague he shared a room nearby at Miss Aldis's house, 71 Gower Street, now the Regency House Hotel, opposite RADA.

During this period he lived (according to his colleague) a peaceful existence doing paperwork in office hours and reading philosophy by night. It's true that, thanks to the uniform and the medals, he tended to be the darling of all the French girls in Soho, and the two friends spent a fair amount of time there. The decorations even won him admittance to theatres and music-halls free of charge: they got to know actresses like Alice Delysia and even on one occasion dined with Mata Hari in her room at the Savoy (their instructions at the Passport Office were to give her a visa eventually but to keep her guessing).

This pleasant life lasted for six months or so, after which Céline was discharged from the army and left both the Passport Office and Gower Street – but not London. It was during this second period, lasting rather less than the first, that he collected the material for the extraordinary *Guignol's Band*, Parts 1 and 2. He now, it seems, said goodbye to officialdom without much regret and divided his time between Leicester Square and the East End. From his base at 4 Leicester Street – not then a respectable Chinese restaurant as it is today – he threw in his lot with a motley crowd of pimps, prostitutes and drug-pedlars. Though neglecting his philosophy, he seems to have had a happy time, for there is much poetry in the *Guignol's Band* books. The East End, for instance, he finds full of fair-haired children, who dance and sing to barrel-organs at the corner of every street. And then there is the Thames nearby. 'If only all roads were rivers,' he sighs. And there is the scene in the garden when the fair-haired Virginia tells him she is pregnant and the French text is spattered with English words of great tenderness: 'Dear, what is it? . . . You sure? . . . I think . . . What age are you? . . . Fourteen . . . Who told you, darling? . . . The doctor . . . Doctor? You been? when? . . . Last night . . . Little one, little one, you sure? . . . Yes, yes . . . Then I don't go. I'll never leave you. Now go to bed, dear, go to bed. We'll see tomorrow. Tomorrow, little one. Tomorrow.'

It is fairly clear that Céline did have a serious love affair in London, which left him full of remorse. There are odd mentions of it in at least two of the books, and signs that he never forgave himself. No details are known; but it is on record that on 16 January 1916 Lieutenant Louis Destouches (his real name) strolled across from Leicester Street to the register office in Covent Garden (15 Henrietta Street, next to Gollancz, the publishers) and there married Suzanne Nebout of Marble Arch Mansions, of whom nothing else is ever heard.

The Devil and T.S.E.

he Belgian poet Jean de Boschère (1878–1953) never really set the Scheldt on fire, but his story is of special interest to the English.

When he fled to London, as a refugee, in January 1915, he had yet to make his mark. By good luck, however, he had been corresponding with F. S. Flint, who now became his guide in London. Their first port of call was Harold Monro's Poetry Bookshop, then situated a few steps south of Queen's Square, Bloomsbury. (The spot is marked today by an Italian restaurant.) Here he was introduced to Richard Aldington, H. D. and all the other Imagists – but especially to Ezra Pound.

De Boschère was a quick learner, and Pound, as ever, the great persuader. In the intervals of teaching at a boys' school in Greenwich the Belgian poet was initiated into all the secrets of Imagism. It was in an abandoned garden near his flat in Tresillian Road, Brockley, that he began writing poems for Pound, and though the garden itself featured in many of them, the mood was not Georgian:

> Yet I am alone in this orchard
> With pencil and paper,
> With this old hat which has seen Naples and Amsterdam
> London and Cologne . . .

> Yet I am alone in this orchard
> With this old hat that saw Naples and Pisa,
> With an apple-tree blossoming in white and pink,
> And all its branches breaking into urgent laughter.

The Closed Door, which appeared in September 1917 with illustrations by the author, was an Imagist book if ever there was one: opposite the French originals were English versions supplied by his London guide F. S. Flint. But the most puzzling thing was that often these poems bore a striking resemblance to the work of T. S. Eliot, as in the following excerpt from 'Homer Marsh':

> For four seasons Homer travels,
> And in each town he is another person:
> Blue beneath a blue sky, grey in London,
> Composed in Paris, corrupt in Rome
> Amid the order of the tomb of tombs;
> Byron in the Aegean, and Shakespeare again
> In Rome's dust of men.
> But never is he Marsh.

But literary subtleties did not concern the forthright critic James Douglas, who in the *Star* of 19 October 1917 described de Boschère as the Devil incarnate:

He is the last word in decadent symbolism, imagism, futurism, cubism or whatever infernal ism you please. He is more clammily horrible than Tchekhov or Reinhardt or any of the slimy reptiles that used to shimmer in the Russian Ballet.

'Devilish, most devilish', was the critic's parting shot, of which remark the poet's friend André Suarez was quick to seize the significance. 'This man is not your enemy,' he wrote perceptively. 'He could hardly have served you better!' And in fact the book became overnight the talk of London and in no time at all the opportunistic author – encouraged no doubt by his astute publisher John Lane of *Yellow Book* fame – had assumed the role in which Douglas had cast him. He began to dress up in sinister suits of black or purple velvet with matching accessories. When he walked down Piccadilly, sometimes carrying a lantern to warn the populace, little children were snatched out of his reach – but at the same time society hostesses competed ruthlessly to have him at their *soirées*. And a journalist from *The Times* wrote: 'What a gracious, well-groomed, debonair Devil it is! This is the most distinguished Devil I know of, superior in every way to Mr Bernard Shaw.'

However, in the *Dial* of January, Conrad Aiken wrote: 'In all likelihood Mr Eliot's "Love Song of J. Alfred Prufrock" would not have been the remarkable thing it is, if it had not been for the work of Jean de Boschère.' It was a fatal judgement and almost certainly wrong, although *Prufrock and Other Observations* and *The Closed Door* had both been published in the course of the same year (1917). Ever afterwards de Boschère bore a grudge: he became convinced that T. S. Eliot had stolen his thunder. Had he not, after all, stolen Laforgue's? And so, on the occasion of Eliot's Nobel Prize in 1949 he did not hesitate to make the suggestion quite openly. Eliot's French translator Pierre Leyris, while agreeing that certain resemblances 'leapt to the eye', refused to go further. Eliot himself kept silent.

And now we have de Boschère's official biography, recently published in Belgium, and Christian Berg settles the matter once and for all: neither poet copied the other, they merely went to the same sources of inspiration (in 'Homer Marsh', the source being clearly Corbière), and they had the same mentor: *il miglior fabbro* himself.

De Boschère

Piccadilly

Maurice Sachs: the London connection

xcellent writer and self-confessed brigand, Maurice Sachs (1906-45) is famous for his posthumous best-seller *Le Sabbat* (Witches' Sabbath), subtitled 'the Memoirs of a Misspent Youth'.

Sachs had many connections with England, beginning with his nurse Susan, who taught him the language and whom he used to disconcert greatly by his nightly prayer: that he might wake up next morning as a little girl. It had apparently been the wish also of his mother Andrée, who was related to that Proustian character Mme Straus, one of the originals of the Duchesse de Guermantes. Maurice's first crisis came with the war of 1914 when he was evacuated to England with the mother he hardly knew. He fell in love, however, with London, which provided his first aesthetic memory: a street scene as vivid as a Peter de Hooch.

It was to London that he returned in 1923, again with his mother who, pursued by creditors, had to find refuge anywhere outside France. Throughout that summer the 16-year-old boy worked in the foreign book department of John and Edward Bumpus Ltd, then at 350 Oxford Street, on the corner of Marylebone Lane. He describes spending most of the time comforting Andrée in their little flat in Campden Hill Gardens – but this did not prevent him going back to France in October and never seeing her again.

According to Sachs, the firm of Bumpus had offered him a five-year contract as head of the department on condition that he took out British nationality. Before doing so he consulted a friend of the family, René Blum, collector and balletomane, the lightweight brother of Léon. Nicknamed 'Le Blumet', René was the man who introduced Marcel Proust to his publisher Bernard Grasset. He ordered Maurice to return to Paris forthwith: it was unpatriotic to change one's nationality, even if the other country happened to be England.

Now began Sachs' real career. Jean Cocteau had just lost his beloved Radiguet, so Maurice resolved to take his place. It was a hopeless ambition but for a time, as Cocteau's secretary, he believed it might come true. At a revival of *Romeo and Juliet* he even played the page to Cocteau's Mercutio. Then books began to disappear, and Maurice may not have been responsible. Cocteau, who liked thieves far better then policemen, made light of it: books were never stolen, they were simply 'borrowed'. But Maurice's true nature had to reveal itself eventually: he began the long string of shady deals involving books, paintings, antiques, gold, currency etc, which he never denied more than half-heartedly. When Misia Sert, after a dinner party, frisked his overcoat and found two priceless spoons he could only murmur: 'You were quite right to be suspicious. With me one never knows . . .'

Perhaps in an effort to reform himself he became involved with Jacques Maritain and his Russian wife Raïssa, who specialized in converting the French intelligentsia of the time – they even had the Pope's permission to install a private chapel in their Meudon property. Never one to do anything by halves, Maurice was not only converted, he joined a Left

Bank seminary where he was known to one and all as Monsieur l'Abbé. But this phase ended when (according to popular legend which he hotly denies in the book) he stripped off his *soutane* on the beach at Juan-les-Pins to reveal a pink bathing dress. This was 1926, Juan's first season as a summer resort, so the incident could hardly go unnoticed.

The years 1930–33 were spent in America, where in the course of a protracted lecture tour he met and married a lady in the mid-West, but somehow or other returned to France with a boyfriend called Henry. After this he exercised his charm mainly in literary circles: André Gide and his colleagues at the NRF were less taken in than most, but they suffered him quite gladly and gave him work from time to time. In 1937 he emerged unexpectedly as the co-translator of Terence Rattigan's *French without Tears*, and the success of this piece induced him to think his future lay in the theatre. In November of that year he even brought a troupe to London, where he stayed at Claridge's and made himself as conspicuous as possible, half hoping perhaps that his mother might emerge from the shadows to claim him. But this last visit to London was a flop and he returned to Paris with one thing on his mind: to write his autobiography, a job he completed admirably, and it was only the outbreak of war that frustrated publication. Selling all interests in the book outright to his publishers, he now gave full attention to the war in progress.

As it was still the 'phoney' war he joined the British forces as interpreter at Cherbourg, where his main occupation seems to have been liaising with the local brothels. But as the war itself changed key, so his own life lurched from farce into tragedy. He became heavily involved in the Black Market and all the other intrigues of the Occupation. Was it to escape his creditors that he fled to Germany (just as his mother had fled to England)? Is it true that his one good deed (taking pity on a Jesuit priest who worked for the Resistance) led inexorably to his own downfall? Facts are few but he was finally jailed, it seems, for the ironic crime of betraying the Gestapo. And when the Allies approached his Hamburg prison in 1945, he was marched off with the other prisoners in the direction of Kiel. Unable to keep up with the column, he was shot at the roadside by an SS guard on 14 April.

Next year in Paris his publisher (Correa) finally brought out *Le Sabbat*, which was a runaway success. The book contains a heartfelt cry, which may or may not have been sincere: '*Maman*, if you read this book, please believe that I always felt the most real feelings of devotion for you, even if they were sometimes hidden.'

Maman did read the book – how could she not? For this time Maurice had made his mark. She went to Paris and met the publisher. Then she collected from far and wide – from casual friends and former creditors – all the unpublished manuscripts of her son, which became published successes in the years that followed. The books continued to appear for fifteen years after his death.

Simone Weil

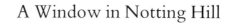

A Window in Notting Hill

Philosopher-Saint or Revolutionary-Mystic? Simone Weil was certainly the most unusual of the Free French visitors to London during the Second World War.

Not for her the little clubs of St James's: her style could hardly be more austere. Her ideal, in fact, was to exist on the same material level as the poorest of Europe's wartime poor.

She worked for de Gaulle at 19 Hill Street, Mayfair, commuting between Marble Arch and Holland Park on the Central Line. All that is known about her life outside office hours is what she wrote in letters to her parents.

She arrives in England at the end of 1942, and on 31 December she writes that the two principal traits of the English are humour and kindness, but especially kindness. She has observed it constantly, she says, in little scenes of everyday life.

On 22 January she announces: 'I've found a room: the landlady is charming.'

On 1 February: 'I like London more and more. My room is in the Notting Hill district, c/o Mrs Francis, 31 Portland Road, W11. It's a very pretty room right at the top of the house. Just outside my window there's a tree whose branches are full of birds – and at night of stars.'

For the record it was a back room, looking on to Princedale Road – from which vantage point it is the top-right window of the last house.

A month later she says: 'My landlady is the widow of a school-teacher who died about ten years ago, leaving her with two boys to bring up: a four-year-old (David) and a baby (John). She had no means of earning a living, and no resources except this little house. The whole thing is pure Dickens. I now understand that the ordinary people of England are exactly as he depicted them. Surprisingly it's his sentimental side, which the French find so false, that is absolutely true.'

Simone Weil lived with Mrs Francis for only three months. On 15 April she was transferred to a private room in Middlesex Hospital, from which she moved to a nursing home in the country, dying later that year, aged 34, at least partly from self-inflicted privations.

M. Butor's Landlady

One of the most unhappy Frenchman ever to reach these islands was Michel Butor, the author of *L'Emploi du Temps*, the *nouveau roman* about Manchester.

As Dr F. Whitehead has remarked, M. Butor writes of a Manchester transformed into something that Mancunians will hardly recognize: a forbidding dark wood in whose mazes the hero wanders disconsolately. 'The air is tainted with sulphur, and the River Slee (no doubt a transcription of the Irwell stagnating between warehouses) traverses it like some stream of Hades. Few novels convey better the loneliness of the stranger in a strange land.'

Although M. Butor taught for two years (1951-53) at the French department of Manchester University, his ex-colleagues seem unwilling to be drawn on the subject. The furthest one of them would go was: *C'était un personnage plus près de Kafka que de Proust.*

It is therefore pleasant to be able to record that, in the course of writing a fascinating thesis for the same university, J. B. Howitt made a remarkable discovery: Butor's landlady.

Readers of M. Butor's novel will remember her as Mrs Grosvenor – named apparently after the author's favourite cinema, the Grosvenor, at All Saints'. In the book she is so reactionary that, though she has been warmly recommended by the hero's black friend, he prefers to stay out of reach for fear of incurring her righteous wrath: he knows only too well that to her he is just another of those 'black devils'.

In real life, she had many virtues, and her name was Mrs N. Ward, of 41 Southbank Road, Manchester 19 — a semi-detached council house, just off the Kingsway dual-carriageway. By the time of Mr Howitt's visit she was 94 and rather deaf, but it became clear that she and the author had got along well together.

M. Butor, it seems, used to write in her living room in the evenings after dinner. She did not realize what it was he was writing – actually it was his first novel, *Passage de Milan* – but she suggested to him once or twice that he 'must be a Communist or something', for this also seemed indicated by his not going to church on Sundays. However, she did not labour the point – and it was a funny thing, her feelings began to change: even though he was a foreigner, he seemed a good sort.

Once when he was ill, Mrs Ward put on her hat and walked all the way to the university; she wanted to tell the professors that he really *was* ill and not just pretending. Another time there was that trouble with the lodger, the difficult one – she'd really got worked up that time, but the man was a fool: he'd been in the first war and didn't much care for Frenchmen. In fact he couldn't stomach them and one day told her that M. Butor would have to go. But Mrs Ward had a surprise for him: it was *he* who went: M. Butor remained – with extra Bovril at nights.

If ever the neighbours criticized his manner of dress (heavy crepe-soled shoes) or the way he did his hair (the crew-cut of those times) Mrs Ward would fly to his defence. In fact she tried in her modest way to guide his path through the maze of Manchester life – a sort of Lancashire Ariadne – and though he did not finally carry her off in his ship, there is no doubt he appreciated her help in a town he heartily detested.

It is, of course, rash to jump to conclusions about a *nouveau roman*, but it does seem from internal evidence that the city of Manchester – or 'Bleston' as he calls it – reduced M. Butor to something of a wreck. How else to explain the relentless monotony of all those relative clauses piled one on the other like the House-that-Jack-built of a mad professor? It is true, too, that the first thing he did on leaving the place was to be operated on for ulcers.

Yet it is possible that M. Butor today, in his house on the French Riviera, looks back on the experience with a certain quiet satisfaction, if not nostalgia. For, by a strange and wonderful irony, it was the hated Manchester – strained through the pages of *L'Emploi du Temps* – that brought him fame and fortune.

Bleston is not a very nice name to give a town – it sounds like a blister on a blasted heath - so the idea of M. Butor having a soft spot for the place might seem fanciful. But here is a fact: some years later, when he was about to get married, he was careful to send Mrs Ward a formal announcement. And Mrs Ward? Though delighted, she passed it off with a shrug - perhaps the man wasn't a Communist after all.

Other Adventures

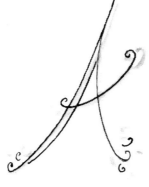

Famous People I (almost) Met

t an impressionable age I was urged by my father to start a notebook called 'Famous people I have met'. I went next door and met our neighbour, a famous actor called Herbert Marshall. What next?

After that there was a lull. For weeks Mr Marshall's name was the only one in the book. So we decided to relax the rules: henceforth it would be acceptable if I only *saw* the famous person from a distance . . . or perhaps met one of his relations . . . or got a letter from him.

Looking back I can see how this has influenced my life: I am drawn towards famous people in a vague way, without really needing to meet them.

On holiday the next year in Dieppe I saw Sir Gerald du Maurier, and took a snapshot of him as he disappeared under the Tourelles arch on the sea-front. Having sent the picture to him with my compliments, I sat back and waited for the thank-you letter. When it did not come, my father explained that we might have been tactless: perhaps he was visiting Dieppe incognito, not officially there at all. I was learning about life.

The next famous person I didn't actually meet was Eddie Marsh, Churchill's secretary and sponsor of the Georgian poets. I had fallen under the spell of a painting called 'The Cornfield' by John Nash. It had been quite widely reproduced, with the mention that it was in the Collection of Mr Marsh. My father thought it best to write to him direct: if everything came out right I would be able to add the Collector himself to my collection of famous men. This I did, and received a note: 'By all means come and see it. Sorry I can't be here myself, but my servant will let you in and show you the picture – and any others you may care to see.'

When I called at 5 Raymond Buildings, Gray's Inn, I was greeted warmly by a nice old lady, who showed me the paintings with the aplomb of a curator. There were so many that they crowded all the walls right up to the ceiling, and both sides of the doors which rattled when you opened them. Even then there was too little space: Mr Marsh asked the housekeeper to choose a selection for her own room to help disperse them. She had chosen nothing but images of food in various guises. There were dead pheasants and still-lifes of apples in profusion. On our way through the rooms I noticed that she made no reference to the photographs of Ivor Novello, Rupert Brooke and other romantic young men dotted about – perhaps they weren't part of the Collection. At the end of the visit I felt I knew Eddie Marsh quite well without ever having met him: he was obviously a kind gentleman who had earned the love of countless young men, and of his charming housekeeper.

In the pursuit of famous people all the fun seemed to be in travelling, and it wasn't really necessary to arrive. When I discovered the little teashop at 6 Holland Street, W8, where Imagism was invented in April 1912, Richard Aldington was no longer there, but the place was eloquent in its way. And I did nearly catch up with Aldington the following month, when I found I was following him through France. I got nearest in Brantôme, which he had left only the previous evening. The hotel proprietor, Madame Roy, gave me a satisfactory word-picture of how the author spent the day writing, while his secretary (Brigit Patmore?) typed on the balcony. When *Life Quest* appeared I felt that the elegiac passage beginning: 'Below the crooked bridge at Brantôme/ The water of the Dronne runs clear and cold . . .' had been written especially for me – though what he had written in Mme Roy's Livre d'Or was more concerned with 'the stream's pollution and the motorists' senseless hooting'. Perhaps if I had actually met my favourite author I should have found him in an angry mood.

Which brings me to a day in 1938 when, at the American Student Center in the boulevard Raspail, I met a Mrs Adam who told me that her 'nephew wrote too'. Like any journalist in these circumstances I cringed. Surely she was about to ask me for my advice: what should the little lad do next? I soon found, however, that Mrs Adam's nephew did not need advice from me or anyone: he was George Orwell. Mrs Adam, it seemed, was a younger sister of Ida Blair, Orwell's mother. Married to a Monsieur H. K. Adam, a translator, she now lived in Paris and her other name, Nellie, suited her well, for she was a warm, vivacious woman who had once been on the stage. She had already been in Paris at the time that Orwell was living rough at 6 rue du Pot de Fer, working in the kitchens of the Hôtel Lotti and observing death at the Hôpital Cochin. At any moment she would have been at his disposal, glad to help out and be of use. She would not, of course, have fitted into the book he was writing.

As I was leaving, Mrs Adam asked me if I'd care to use a villa they had in North Africa. If I'd said yes, I suppose I might have met Orwell. (Was this perhaps the villa 'near Marrakech' that he mentions somewhere?) True to my principles, however, I declined. Why bother to meet him? I had him in the book.

George Orwell

Beatrice and the Wasp

As a specialist in almost meeting famous men, I was delighted recently to meet the son of Orage, that great editor who doesn't need initials. And an extra bonus was that, buried in the files of the old *New Age*, I found many treasures – for instance, the discovery of Italy by Richard Aldington, from 13 February to 10 July 1913. Fascinating, too, is the account by Beatrice Hastings of her love affair with Modigliani.

Apart from using the dewy pseudonym of 'Alice Morning', Mme Hastings made no attempt to disguise the actual events as they occurred in Paris 1914-5. Written on a Monday and published on Thursdays, her sixty or more pieces are still lively to read.

Perhaps the Paris correspondent of a London periodical is always allowed a certain licence (in that role I perpetrated over 200 such pieces) but I can think of no editor before or since who has permitted his employee to give a first-person report of the seduction of a great artist.

Beatrice Hastings may not have been altogether confident in discriminating a hawk from a handsaw, but at her best she is not a bad journalist. The way she presents Life with Modi, set against a background of the Battle of the Marne, may not be in the class of Stendhal, but it does have a distinctive panache. The story opens with a typical street-scene on her arrival in Paris:

I have seen the French children. They are adorable. A little duck passed me by the Madeleine and held up one finger. I laughed and winked, and when we both looked back she came running to ask me to go to the dancing. The governess told me she was five, but she looked too enchanted, I think, ever to have been ordinarily born. (21 May 1914)

Then on 4 June 1914 we get this laconic observation: 'I saw a wedding this morning, poor things. She looked charmingly cross.'

Enter Modigliani (4 June 1914) as a 'pale and ravishing villain' in 'cap, scarf and corduroy'. On 11 June they go to the cinema. ' "Ah, j'adore ça," he said, and never looked at a single scene. "You mustn't go to sleep on my shoulder," I objected, "all the world knows you." "Not a soul," he said and waved anew to somebody else. "You mustn't fall in love with me," he said. "Don't be ridiculous," I said, "*you're* much more likely." '

An argument about the douanier Rousseau (9 July 1914) is duly reported: 'What beats me is when an unsentimental artist like Modigliani says of Rousseau "Oui, très joli." I would like to buy one of the Italian's stone heads, but he is liable to *give* you anything you look interested in. "Nothing's lost," he says, and bang goes another drawing. He is a very beautiful person to look at, always either laughing or quarrelling. If only he hadn't said that thingamy was très joli. He horrifies some English friends of mine whose flat overlooks his studio by tubbing at two-hour intervals in the garden. Speaking of studios mine is a duck with two rooms and real running water. My concierge is also a duck, and everything's very joyful except a large rat which is a shocking thief.'

Modi was soon sharing the studio at 53 rue du Montparnasse, rat and all. But on 16 July she has to visit England: 'I didn't know what to do with M. on the station when he fainted loudly against the grubby side of the carriage, gasping, "Oh Madame, don't go." So I said, "Modigliani, someone says you've been three years fiddling about with one type of head . . ." He glared at me: "Mais ma petite, he is right. I might have grown asparagus in the time." '

Soon after her return their Montparnasse idyll is interrupted (but not too much) by the Great War. Alice Morning finds herself coping (10 September) with the Battle of the Marne:

Everybody except me went today to see the cattle and sheep in the Bois de Boulogne. Thousands, they say, have been brought in from the fields outside the fortifications, where the soldiers have already dug trenches. I went with a friend to Notre Dame, which was sacredly quiet and cool as paradise.

Food and money became scarce at the Rotonde, and the effects are observed: 'The misery is so quiet that you may sit next to it quite a while before catching that dreadful gesture of the hand to the dizzy head . . . When I say that the concierges like one woman chase away from the courtyards starving singers and musicians, many of whom a few weeks ago were employed in the cabarets on the boulevards, I only give a faint hint of the universal and systematic suppression of everything but grief and grocery.' (8 October 1914)

Modi is still around – but so is the flu. 'Sitting' in the nude becomes a hazard: 'Somebody has done a lovely drawing of me. I look like the best type of Virgin Mary, without any worldly accessories as it were. But what do I care about it now – my career is nothing but a sneeze.' (5 November) Modi falls ill too : 'I've been indoors nursing a sick wasp. The wasp strays in, eats a little honey, tries to sting and then crawls out to some winter lair. I suspect it is more sleepy than sick.' (11 February 1915)

Death itself is just round the corner: 'My good friend, the hostess of the Hôtel Blois, rue Vavin, has lost her eldest son. Twice wounded, he went to the trenches for the third time and was killed. She will never again be the same bright creature, but she does not cease any the less to console the rest of the world.' (25 February)

Beatrice now moves to the cottage at II bis rue Norvins at Montmartre, scene of some odd parties. And the chatter goes on: 'I wonder if anyone has any right to talk about themselves as much as I do? I can't believe it, and yet I can't stop. After all, oneself is the only person who remains friendly in spite of all life's little ironies. I took myself out this morning in a murderous mood, and brought myself back quite willing to wipe off old scores and start again.' (5 August 1915) But she is falling out of love with Paris: 'Speaking of concierges makes me want to swear: they are nothing but police spies. I have had no fewer than eight guests this evening, and the old witch at the gate has grumbled at every one of them. Yet she will smile without a blush tomorrow, after I have given her a franc.' (6 May 1915) And on 30 September: 'I think that the Parisians en masse are very stupid. You have no idea what courage it needs to enunciate such a statement: they will have it against me for ever and ever. If in fifty years I may invite the President to a cup of tea, his secretary will say to him: 'That is the woman who said

we were very stupid' – and the President will not come.'

Modigliani has departed, and the magic with him. On 19 August she makes a solemn statement:

Who that has loved would exchange the exaltation of transient love for permanent affection? Not I for one, however transient the first. And we must not try and twist the meaning of things by changing their names, calling domestic affection love, or the lovers will laugh at us.

Fairly soon after this Orage stopped the letters. He knew as well as anyone when a series had to end.

The Candlesticks of M. Radiguet

he emergence of Raymond Radiguet's *Diable au corps* as a French academic text is a well-deserved consecration. It also brings back poignant memories of myself as a teenager in pre-war Arcachon.

I remember, for instance, that elegant *librairie* – bookshop is too prosaic a term – which displayed in its window a glossy magazine, lying open at a Francis Carco article datelined 'Le Piquey':

We reign like kings on a veranda that smells of pine-needles roasted in the sun. Behind three dunes, whose only imprint is mine of yesterday, the Ocean thunders. My dogs bathe and I bathe. There in the sun I seem to lie back on Time itself.

Well, this sounded much more interesting than where I was, so I asked the bookseller where such a paradise could be found. Le Piquey, he said, was on the other side of the 'Bassin'. If I thought of going there, I had only to take the little steamer: he could recommend the Auberge Chantecler and its proprietor Mme Dourthe.

When I got there I found I was the only visitor. It was May and the season hadn't begun. The Chantecler was a two-storey building of wood, a kind of big green bungalow with its name in gold letters strung out along the balcony. As for Mme Dourthe, she was a short stocky woman with black hair, flimsy black skirt and pink *chemise Lacoste* (the then-equivalent of a T-shirt).

Mme Dourthe and I were the sole occupants of the Auberge Chantecler. At night, when she turned over in bed on the floor below, I could feel the whole building heave and creak. When she cooked my delicious meals she would after-wards come and sit at my table on the veranda. Under our feet was a carpet of pine-needles, and one evening she men-tioned casually that Monsieur Cocteau had always called it 'la litière' (i.e. the litter that farm animals lie on). At the sound of the word Cocteau my mind sprang to attention, 'Why yes, M. Cocteau was often here. But not since M. Radiguet died.'

At the time I don't think I had heard of Radiguet, but during a fortnight of meal-time conversations Mme Dourthe told me everything there was to know. We also played the records that Cocteau had left behind, and I tried to imagine him and Radiguet dancing the quadrille from *Orphée aux Enfers* at breakfast-time. Then I pictured them at the barber's, where Cocteau would reverently (the word is Mme Dourthe's) gather up the fallen locks of his friend. As a special privilege I had even been allotted Radiguet's bed-room, where Cocteau locked him in to keep him working on the book – a book which Mme Dourthe had not actually read but greatly respected.

Francis Carco in the glossy magazine had not exaggerated the beauty of the spot. The collection of huts called Le Piquey was situated on a long, narrow spit of sandy pine forest between the Bassin d'Arcachon and the Atlantic Ocean. The Auberge itself had its toes in the Bassin, where all was serene and quiet and where the oyster cages gently

Balanos. At a certain hour of the evening the light was such that you seemed to be living in a pearl.

At the end of my holiday I was sad to leave. So indeed was Mme Dourthe to see me go. On the last morning, before accompanying me to the boat, she offered me a little something to remember her by: a pair of ornate Empire candelabra which had been left behind by Cocteau. Alas, the little something turned out to be much too heavy to carry away. Pity, but those candlesticks weighed a ton!

Years later I returned to Le Piquey – as one always does and so mistakenly. Mme Dourthe had gone but – worse than that – I could not find anyone who remembered her. Neither could I recognize Le Piquey. In the meantime, though, I had transferred my affections to Radiguet's book, and the Literary Editor of the Paris *L'Aurore* had even taken me to Le Parc-Saint-Maur, Radiguet's birthplace and the setting of his novel. It had been a lightning spin in a sports car, after which I longed for a more leisurely look, with perhaps a more sympathetic guide. As it happened my luck was in: the guide I finally found was Radiguet's own young brother René, who still lived in the district.

Le Parc-Saint-Maur is a south-eastern suburb of Paris – a riverside suburb with something of the atmosphere of Richmond, enclosed in a great bend of the slow-moving Marne. In one of his notebooks Radiguet wrote:

Those who know the Marne know that the sweetness of this river is incomparable. Its waters surpass all others in gentleness . . . We lived at Le Parc-Saint-Maur. I was born there and never really left it. The word 'park' seemed so right. I was an animal in that park. I roamed there like a deer, and never for a moment felt sad or imprisoned.

Le Diable au corps is a love story of the Marne. Its heroine is not only Marthe but the Marne, and on a certain spring day René Radiguet literally led me through the décor of his brother's novel, pointing out the leafy suburban villas where one or other of the characters had lived – for the book is based fairly closely on real life and the setting here – unlike Le Piquey – had not greatly changed with the years. When I told him about Le Piquey René seemed quite interested, but not till I mentioned the candelabra was he visibly moved. Then, without saying much, he led me back to his house, where he unearthed a letter that Raymond had written him from Chantecler:

My dear René,
Could you ask Papa to send me the pair of candelabra that are in the room that used to be mine – and to pack them up safely. This will sound a funny request but candles are the only lighting we have at Le Piquey and – to be able to write in the evening – one needs simply regiments of them. So those candelabra would really help us out – otherwise we have to go to bed like chickens as soon as it's dark!
Raymond R.

'Do you think I could find that lady?' René asked me as we walked to the station. 'I would so love to see those candlesticks again.' I said I'd put some kind of appeal. So if you are still alive, Mme Dourthe, here is the message from René Radiguet: he would like those candlesticks, please, and is prepared to pay the postage.

submerged and reappeared again according to the tides. But a brisk walk through the pines brought you to a very different scene: M. Carco's thundering ocean and endless sands, where he exercised the dogs.

The smell of resin was everywhere, and Mme Dourthe even cooked on a fire of pine-cones. No wonder her long, deep breathings – followed by a 'Ça me fait du *bieng*!' – were so frequent and so irresistible. The surrounding villages had Greek-sounding names like Andernos, Mios, Biganos,

My Life with Picasso

Seeing Paloma on television the other day reminded me of the time she walked over a fat Frenchman on the beach at Collioure. 'Little brat!' he had cried, or its equivalent in demotic French. But when told it was Picasso's child he weakly waited for her to do it again.

The year was 1954, the month September. I had taken a late summer holiday and, after spending some time in Perpignan listening to *sardanes* in the Palmarium, I had pushed on to Collioure in the hope of a few last summer bathes in the Mediterranean.

I had never been to Collioure before, so I turned in at the Café des Sports, a typical enough place with the zinc bar just inside the doorway to the left. Sitting there on a stool and sipping a drink of the day called Suze, I let my eyes wander. Behind the rows of apéritif bottles there was a mirror and, reflected in it, a red banquette, occupied at the moment by a noisy group of Spaniards. Amused by their antics, I turned to look at them and did a double-take, having recognized in one of them the well-known features of Picasso. It was my first inkling that he was in these parts, his usual habitat being the Côte d'Azur, some two hundred miles to the east.

So I got talking to the owner of the place, one René Pous, who told me that the great man had only recently discovered Collioure, which was extraordinary when you considered that it was the painters' village par excellence, made famous in the early years of the century by those Fauves, or wild beasts, Matisse and Derain. Picasso, it seemed, had lately grown tired of being mobbed on the streets of the Riviera and welcomed the comparative peace of Roussillon. But another reason for his presence, I soon learnt, was Rosita, who at that moment was one of the joyous Spaniards on the banquette.

Rosita was the adopted daughter of his old friend Totote Hugué, who in turn was the widow of the sculptor Manolo (Manuel Hugué). The two women lived at nearby Céret, the village that had been associated with the beginnings of Cubism, but they had temporarily joined the Picasso entourage who were camped out in some of the fifty rooms of the magnificent town house of the Comte and Comtesse de Lazerme at Perpignan. Every day the caravan – headed by Picasso's chauffeur-son Paulo – travelled to Collioure to join the painter's smaller children: Claude, aged seven, and Paloma, five. They were staying with their nanny chez Pous – and it was thus I found that M. Pous also ran a hotel, the Hostellerie des Templiers, where I promptly booked in.

It did not take long to notice that everything revolved round Rosita: the whole crazy whirl of activity was in her honour. It seemed that earlier that year the mother of Claude and Paloma (Françoise Gilot) had left Picasso for good, but had allowed him to borrow the children for the summer. He now looked happy enough and as brown as a berry, but actually he was sad. Most of the people around him seemed to be hoping that the place left vacant by Françoise would be taken by the dark, attractive Rosita. The locals perhaps wished this for rather dubious reasons, for if Picasso fell for Rosita, he might then settle in the Roussillon and bring great prosperity to the region (just then groping its way towards tourism after a desperate battle with mosquitoes). So it was not entirely fortuitous that Picasso began to receive offers of fabulous châteaux, such as the early sixteenth-century Fort Saint-Elme, which the locals hoped he would decorate and make famous, as he had done with the one at Antibes. Political passions and great fury were aroused when the local council appeared to be dragging its feet and the project became bogged down in bureaucratic mire.

But everything depended really on Rosita and when the poor girl seemed to hesitate she at once became the target of the locals' wrath. Clearly she was a stupid girl, said the old wives of Roussillon. She didn't know a good thing when she saw it. She had better make her mind up soon or else . . .

It was at this juncture, amid all the turmoil, that I introduced myself to Picasso, explaining only that I was English and that long ago, in 1919, he had done a small portrait sketch of my uncle, a friend of Diaghilev. Without hesitation he pronounced my uncle's name (though they hadn't met for thirty-five years) and asked how the sketch was looking. I told him it was barely legible and, again without hesitation, he told me why: 'The colour of the pencil's too near the colour of the paper.' At this traumatic moment in his life he had total recall of a quite unimportant drawing.

Finally Picasso was claimed, almost inevitably it seemed, by the faithful Jacqueline Roque, who was to look after him for the last twenty years of his life (her utter devotion perhaps underlined by her suicide).

At the last bullfight of the season at Céret, Picasso presided, flanked by Totote Hugué on his left, Rosita on his right. Then Françoise came down and collected the children . . . Picasso went back to the Riviera and Jacqueline . . . while I returned to England and the office. It was the end of my life with Picasso.

Mon Oncle

My Uncle Teddy – otherwise known as Edwin Evans junior – was a much larger man than his father, Edwin Evans senior. Though they were both music critics the older man delighted in Brahms, while my uncle preferred the French and Russians. They disagreed so violently about this in print that a third critic (Ernest Newman?) hit upon the only possible solution: Edwin Evans senior must put Edwin Evans junior across his knee and give him a good spanking. This proposal was never carried out: their respective sizes made it impractical.

The problem of size had already come up at the Salzburg meeting of 1922 when the International Society for Contemporary Music, of which my uncle was later to become president, was founded. A dejected young Francis Poulenc was wandering about like a lost soul, having lost his luggage and with it his dress-suit. 'I'd lend you mine but we aren't the same size,' said my uncle ('Nous n'avons pas le même ventre').

It used to be claimed that my uncle had the most famous back-view in London and that the vision of him sailing down the corridors of the old Queen's Hall was one of the sights of the town. According to a contemporary description he was hardly less impressive in repose: 'Wherever he might happen to be sitting he constituted a kingdom of his own. His physical magnitude was compelling enough; even more so the magnanimity with which he would struggle to his feet, a dozen times if necessary, to allow late-comers to pass. He would rise, gather up his cloak and put his enormous Bohemian hat on his head, all without the least complaint. But those obliged to disturb him made a resolution, as they squeezed by, never to be late again.'

He is usually described in the reference books as Diaghilev's musical adviser but he was more than that: in many ways he was the great man's Man Friday, called upon to perform all manner of tasks but especially those calling for subtle diplomacy. Diaghilev would ring him whenever he was in trouble, which often meant in the middle of the night when some minor problem assumed critical proportions. My uncle might protest that he was losing valuable sleep, though he knew that sleep mattered little to Diaghilev. Using his well-known diplomacy Evans at last intimated that there might be other, more personal and delicate reasons for not disturbing his nights. As a man of the world Diaghilev at once took the hint: the nocturnal phone-calls ceased abruptly.

There were, however, other Russian ways of harassing my genial uncle, such as persuading him, much against his better judgement, to go on stage and harangue the audience. This happened at the London first night of Stravinsky's *Rite of Spring* on 11 July 1913. So anxious was Diaghilev to avoid the riotous scenes that had marked the ballet's Paris première that, before raising the curtain, he sent Evans on to soften up the audience. It was an operation that might have been fatal in less sure hands than those of my uncle.

Luckily the incident did nothing to dampen his friendship with Stravinsky, as the composer's letters (which have been flooding the Paris autograph houses these past few years) show: they are addressed to a 'Mon vieux' or 'Mon cher vieux' who would be astounded if he were still around to see the prices they fetch. What delighted him at the time was the way this friendship gave him insight into Stravinsky's music. In his posthumous *Music and the dance* (1948) Evans records one example:

One Sunday afternoon Stravinsky and I took a taxi and, roaming through the deserted City of London, came upon St Paul's just as the bells were pealing. Stravinsky stopped the cab and listened intently to the 'changes', taking occasional notes on the back of an envelope. He was most enthusiastic about the variety of the sequences, in which he claimed to hear the most wonderful music. There is something about Les Noces, *and particularly about its strange concluding pages, that makes me wonder whether, in all essentials, the substance of the music (or at least the percussive element which animates it) was not born in London on that Sunday afternoon a few weeks before the outbreak of the First World War.*

With the passing years I came to realize the advantages of having such a prestigious uncle. Just as I began, for instance, to be interested in ballet he became chairman of the Camargo Society, bringing over stars like Spessivtseva for occasional performances. What impressed me was that he could tell exactly from which part of Russia a Russian dancer came. I tried him out on my friend Vera Volkova, whose provenance he identified instantly as pure 'Pétersbourg'.

I found too that painters were interested in my uncle. Picasso did that portrait sketch of him in 1919, and I have a photograph of him with Pablo, Diaghilev and Olga Koklova, taken (by Massine?) outside the Café de Paris, Monte Carlo, in April 1925.

Then there was the matter of the Wyndham Lewis portrait in oils that I had seen many times at the top of the stairs in my uncle's South Ken flat. I always thought it looked a bit unfinished, but interestingly so. One day Sir Arthur Bliss told me why. It had been commissioned by a group of English composers whose generosity was not quite equalled by their ability to pay the artist's fee. Lewis refused to finish the canvas until he had received payment in full. So a strange dance began: the composers would drum up a few pounds, upon which Lewis would add a few brushstrokes. It dragged on until my uncle at last stepped in and took the painting home, having judged that he had waited exactly long enough. His timing, I believe, was perfect.

Evans had been educated on the Continent and learnt his perfect French at Lille. As a young man in London he tried the Bohemian life but had to give it up for something more remunerative in the City. His friends took this to be the end of a promising career and even staged a mock funeral at which one of the 'pall-bearers' was Oscar Wilde. To their surprise, however, Evans took to the City like a duck to water. Not only did he make a success of his City job but he had moved to an important position with a Continental bank and was actually editing a financial weekly when he once again changed gear, saying goodbye for ever to the serious money for the privilege of being awakened at nights by Diaghilev . . .

As a musical journalist between the wars he was prolific – and no doubt needed to be, in view of his gourmet life-style. His friends' one regret was that he never had the leisure to write his memoirs. He died in harness, his last article (on Shostakovich) appearing on the day of his death: 3 March 1945. A kind of memorial.

The Several Lives of Ronald Searle

roucho Marx called him a genius; in 1971, John Lennon announced that, along with Lewis Carroll, he was one of two people who had exerted the most influence on his life; Tom Wolfe called him the giant of the graphic netherworld; Cecil Day Lewis wrote him a dirge; S. J. Perelman was as devoted to his turn of phrase as he was to his nimbleness of line; and Max Beerbohm wrote him a fan letter . . . just a few of the honours bestowed on Ronald Searle, who recently celebrated both his 65th birthday and fifty witty years in print.

Searle has come a long way since his local paper, the *Cambridge Daily News*, published his first drawing when he was fifteen. The trifle he earned helped to pay for his studies at the Cambridge School of Art – studies in the fiercely academic tradition of Tonks and the Slade, that of unremitting toil combined with minute, surgical observation. As crushingly oppressive as Searle found it at the time, he has since remained grateful for the freedom it gave him to 'play' with his pencil and pen. By the time his studies were interrupted by the outbreak of war, Searle was already well-armed with a precocious grasp of drawing. He served seven years as soldier, and the war – in particular the period of captivity under the Japanese from 1942 to 1945 – provided him with the subject matter and the impetus to apply what he had learned. At the age of twenty-six he emerged from the experience to be swiftly recognized as a remarkable draughtsman with (not suprisingly) an almost oriental feeling for the purity of line. Academic success was soon overtaken by popular success as Searle, in an original and very personal way, merged his academic background with graphic satire and a wickedly sharp eye for the ridiculous.

But to return to the teenager, and the war.

Very much against his will and after forty years of silence on the subject, Ronald Searle agreed to accept a tough assignment for the latter half of 1985 to relive for those who could not know the story, the forty-two months he spent in Japanese captivity. Earlier that year he had presented to the Imperial War Museum four hundred drawings documenting those mostly unphotographed – virtually unrecorded – days during the Japanese invasion of South East Asia. After passing through various stages of conservation (de-acidization of paper, etc.) they went on show to the public in March 1986. To coincide with this exhibition of the unknown Searle, a substantial number of drawings were reproduced facsimile in a lavish volume published by Collins (*To the Kwai – and Back: War Drawings 1939-1945*) featuring not only around 200 pages of reproductions in colour but also about 20,000 words of background text. 'Too many background words for any artist,' says Searle. The story of his days in the Siam jungle and later, imprisonment in Changi gaol, took him over five months to write and his efforts to recall the exact circumstances under which each drawing was made also brought him a miserable five months of almost sleepless nights. In 1943 the young art student found himself involved in one of the most barbarous operations in the history of warfare, the building by prisoners of war of a supply railway to the Burma Front through some of the most hostile terrain and virtually impenetrable jungle known on this earth. Later dubbed the 'Thai-Burma Railway of Death'.

'My formation is rooted, I think, in those days of captivity,' he once said. 'To be precipitated into circumstances of almost total isolation, total brutality, total filth and disgust, and virtual slavery at the age of twenty-three inevitably and indelibly marks one's outlook on anything one relates to afterwards – if you were lucky enough to be counted among those few who had an "afterwards". To wake up many mornings with a thousand miles of jungle between you and the Allies, to find the fellow prisoner on each side of one dead, is more than salutary. One begins to clarify in one's mind the nuances of the word "mortality".'

Most of his fellow prisoners perished in that jungle or later in Changi: what kept Searle alive may have been the determination to carry out his self-appointed task of documenting what was happening, in the hope that one day it would be seen. To do, in fact, what Otto Dix and Goya, in their different ways, had done before him. With the essential difference that Searle was part of the drama and any work had to be done in secret and concealed with the help of his fellow prisoners. Concealed where the Japanese would not think (or care) to look – underneath the body, for instance, of a man dying of cholera.

Ten years ago, in a television interview, one of his friends who survived – the Australian writer Russell Braddon – gave a vivid picture of Ronald Searle at this time in a base camp in Siam, after coming out of the jungle:

When the Line was finished he was a sick boy. I remember that there was nothing much of him, that he was like a baby or a monkey or something. We thought he was dying and we – some of his remaining friends – used to put him out on a ground sheet in the sun. I don't know why, but we felt the sun would do something. He could barely move, and we had no food, he had dysentery, malaria and was covered in running sores, and each day we expected him to die. He was a tough little one, though: he wasn't going to. His mad Heath Robinson mentality got to work and he had us make a bamboo pipe so that when he had to urinate, he didn't soil himself. No one else in those camps had managed to devise their own sewage system. If you can imagine something that weighs six stone or so, is on the point of death and has no qualities of the human condition that aren't revolting, calmly lying there with a pencil and a scrap of paper, drawing, *you have some idea of the difference of temperament that this man has from the ordinary human being.*

The resilience of Ronald Searle was such that, a few months after his final release he was back in England – and this is where I first met him – living in a gleaming white cube of a room at 34 Tite Street, Chelsea, already preparing to embark on a career as a freelance artist. Later he discovered from Oscar's son Vyvyan Holland, that the house (previously number 16) had been the home of the Wilde family and that his own bedsitter (first-floor back) had been Oscar's library. 'That decided me to hone what wit I had, out of basic respect for the shadows on the walls,' said Searle.

We met many times that winter of 1945-46: sometimes in a small restaurant – George's? The Star? I forget now – where Thorn House now rears . . . at Vera Volkova's ballet class in West Street, where Karsavina sometimes looked in to pose her shopping basket . . . a dressing room at the Ambassadors

(*Sweet and Low*) . . . my flat in Covent Garden. A major occasion was taking him to the first night of Roland Petit's Ballets des Champs-Elysées at the Adelphi on 9 April 1946, an event which in some ways may have influenced his career and future life: we belong to the same generation and the famous Kochno-Bérard-Sauguet ballet, *Les Forains*, probably sealed our love of France and the French.

During this time Searle was rapidly becoming famous and sought after. Although the girls of St Trinian's had been created before his capitivity, in 1941, their moment along with the rest of Searle's macabre range of humour came now: pictorial Victoriana was dead and post-war England was ripe for Searle. Between return-bouts of malaria he unleashed his graphic ferocity on the hapless public – and they loved it. Searle was away. He moved to a bigger studio, in 77 Bedford Gardens, on Campden Hill. Before too long he could afford to buy a house a bit further north, and he moved into 32 Newton Road in 1951. His first house, but naturally, no ordinary one. This had been designed by the young Denys Lasdun *c.* 1938, who was already showing some talent for the theatrical. Searle's studio on the whole of the topmost floor had a highly unconventional terrace attached to it, overlooking half of Paddington. As Searle said, if one *had* to overlook half of Paddington this was the way to do it. I remember – wineglass in hand – swaying on that high terrace with a slightly stunned, also happily swaying Searle, a few days after he had moved in with his wife, two children and ten thousand books. Any passing anxiety caused by additional responsibilities turned out to be quite unnecessary, for his life, excellently stage-managed as always, continued to build: one series of his books sold three-quarters of a million copies, he became a publisher in his own right; at Malcolm Muggeridge's insistence he joined The Table of Punch along with John Betjeman and Anthony Powell, and he darted back and forth across the Atlantic on film work in Hollywood and editorial work in New York and London. His career as a 'famous' artist was now unstoppable – until one day he quietly stopped it.

Contrary to much of what has been written about this move, the reasons are not at all obscure: they centred round the encroaching pressures of his non-stop work, his lifestyle and the necessity to pause for the first time since he came out of prison fifteen years before, to quietly reassess exactly the direction in which he was going and how he could best use his talent for graphic satire without squandering it. (He remembered Max Beerbohm telling him, 'I have a *little* talent, but I have used it well . . .'). First he needed to cut out the superfluities and concentrate entirely on exploring the range of his possibilities as an international and not a parochial satirist. For a start he needed to reduce social demands on his time and energy.

Until now, most people have sought the cliché answer and have taken this as Searle 'doing a Gauguin' and he has never, as usual, bothered to correct them. But the fact that Searle takes his art seriously has never meant that he, by any stretch of the imagination, wished to be taken as a 'serious' artist. Searle is, and always has been, a one-hundred percent, single-minded graphic satirist, hypnotized by the unbounded possibilities of visual humour and restlessly pursuing his surgery of the deeper recesses of the anatomy of laughter. Any suggestion that Searle – with uncharacteristic loss of his own sense of humour – has ever thought of taking himself seriously, or of diverting himself from that straight and thorny path of graphic satire is nonsense – and I have it from the horse's mouth.

On 9 September 1961, Searle abandoned everything – his home, family, possessions, career, and arrived in France, penniless, but with a clear intention to start again from zero. His early days in Paris were a complete contrast to the all-demanding popular success he had known in England. 'In 1961 Paris was a good place in which to settle and rethink,' he says. 'The atmosphere was conducive to reflection. I've always felt at home there, and certainly on the Left Bank, more so than in London – which I love. Perhaps because I was born in a university town and learning was always part of the bread and butter. The eternal student in me, I guess. Anyway, so far as the bread and butter was concerned, if you were cold you could work in a café all day over a cup of coffee and if you hadn't got cooking facilities, the local baker would roast a bird for you if the occasion was grand – and Billy Bunter's postal order turned up.'

From 1963 things improved, as I was able to see for myself when I visited him in his fourth-floor flat at 4, rue Antoine-Dubois opposite the old medical school. Also he was with Monica. Monica his companion (and, soon after, his second wife) had been in Paris since 1951. She was English, a stage designer, an imaginative cook, brilliant linguist and apart from feeding him (and friends like me) she was able to do much to smooth the way of Ronald's reshaping of his life and take over most of the inevitable chores. A witty, beautiful and intelligent woman to whom Searle remains devoted, not least for her sense of humour . . .

The flat in the Latin Quarter became their base of operations and for the next fourteen years their working life was divided between Paris, Berlin and New York. Meanwhile French colleagues extended a big welcome to Searle, and it was Jean-Pierre Desclozeaux of the *Nouvel Observateur* who eventually had the idea of founding a society in his honour: 'Les Amis de Ronald Searle', which has the distinction of numbering among its twenty-eight founder members two circus clowns – including a Fratellini. It continues, basically to accept donations for aiding young artists short of necessities for their exhibitions. Later, Jean Adhémar, director of the Cabinet des Estampes, Bibliothèque Nationale, was the moving spirit behind the great retrospective at the BN in 1973, Searle being the first living foreigner to receive such homage – with all three floors of a wing to fill. The French Mint became his stamping ground when the director, Pierre Dehaye, suggested that he become a medallist for them, which he was for ten years. The Mint has now struck some twenty commemorative medals sculpted by Searle, but the first (at their suggestion) was a commemorative medal to Searle himself. Meanwhile over in the Marais, Michel Cassé's presses turn as the exclusive printer for the last twenty years of Searle's two or three hundred editions of lithographs.

The very English Searle's love of France – dating (I like to think) from *Les Forains* – does not exclude a delight in French follies and foibles. His letters never miss the latest delicious absurdity or Gallic mangling of the English language. His judgements on French (and other) artists make one regret that the once-planned *Dictionary of Caricature* was finally shelved as an unnecessary consumer of vital drawing time. Yet despite his obsession with work, Searle must be among the best informed and most well-read of artists. Rising at six to read French, English, American and German publications, not to mention the local and international press, he will move on to type a dozen letters before settling for ten hours at his drawing-board. Drawing of course, with the *left* hand, for this master of the pen is proud to be a 'cack-handed' Fenland yokel, whose ancestors rose extremely slowly out of the local bogs and mists.

A constant student of the history of caricature, Searle has accumulated over the years a large collection of original drawings, beginning with the father of portrait caricature itself, Annibale Carracci (1560-1609). But you will find on his walls only work from the seventeenth, eighteenth and nineteenth centuries – mainly Hogarth, Gillray, Richard Newton, Rowlandson and George Cruikshank. There is nothing of his own on the walls and nothing of his contemporaries (not even his old friend 'Vicky', some hundreds of whose letters he arranged to be conveyed to Philip Larkin for safe-keeping at Hull shortly before the latter's death). His choice comes from the necessity to remain aware of the 'roots' of his art, to be faced every day with substantial works that stand up to familiarity and microscopic examination. 'In the light of which', says Searle, 'much of my work and that of my contemporaries falls flat on its face.'

Among literary friends the late S. J. Perelman held pride of place. The first time they met, in a New York restaurant, Searle asked the waiter to direct him to the 'cloakroom'. Perelman exclaimed, 'My God! That's straight out of Baroness Orczy – where are the passing peasants?' They were friends for life. Although they have known each other since the 1950s, Samuel Beckett and Searle rarely coincide these days, although not too long ago Searle and Monica would travel to Ulm or Berlin for the opening of a German production that Beckett had directed. Searle has much in common with Beckett. Caricature is a weapon against injustice but like Beckett, even at his most savage, Searle never loses what Ben Shahn called his 'infinite toleration and sympathy for the human condition . . . for all those crotchety, malshapen, well-intentioned persons, labouring earnestly, arduously and with infinite difficulty through the barbed-wire entanglements of life, but never questioning their duty to go on.' Even when his feelings are too much involved with his subject, Searle never discards caricature. True, many of his youthful portraits of Japanese soldiers and their prisoners are remarkable for their calm and sympathetic understanding, but the object of that exercise was to present a factual document, nothing more.

To many of his admirers today, Searle means *cats*. A word of explanation here. In the manner of La Fontaine ('Je me sers d'animaux pour instruire les hommes') Searle uses animals for his own ends. He is therefore surprised when he receives fraternal greetings from cat-lovers, for the fact is that he doesn't like moggies but simply finds them a 'convenient international currency'. (If the St Trinian's girls were really Japanese in disguise as some have suggested – though not Searle – the cats are people in drag.) I once suggested to Searle that the French artist Grandville, nineteenth-century illustrator of La Fontaine, might have been his immediate inspiration: but Dr Searle went to the bookshelf and took down a 1618 edition of Della Porta's *De Humana Physiognomia* comparing human and animal character, to show that the process had its roots well back in time. My fear is that

Searle will kill off his cats as ruthlessly as he rubbed out the schoolgirls in 1953, knowing that he hates a subject to drag on until he loses interest. But let him be warned: thousands of his admirers would consider this an affront. Cats is delicate ground . . .

1967 was the year of the first of the Searle cat books. It was also the year he and Monica married at the British Embassy, Paris. The five guests who were let into the secret that evening at their friend Pierrette's restaurant, Gachoucha, included one English journalist: me. In the end the 1960s had not gone badly: the initial crisis was followed by recovery as Searle did his planned re-thinking and moved on. But the decade ended on a sombre note. Monica's New Year's Eve present was the news that she had cancer – and a deadly one at that. Three months would see her out, it seemed. She chose to become a privileged front-line guinea-pig for Professor Léon Schwarzenberg, and off they went into the experiment.

For a while I moved over to Paris to be of some use as a telephone answering service: Searle either lived at, or dashed back and forth from, the hospital. That was many long medical years ago. But the Searles and Léon (now a firm friend) still meet to crack a bottle of champagne over the result that also led other sufferers out of the condemned cell.

Inevitably this challenge changed – once more – the pattern of Searle's life, but although the 1970s became the years of cliff-hanging for them both, with little travel and fewer encounters with their friends, their semi-isolation in the heart of Paris during the seemingly everlasting treatment provided them with a bridge to their next (unexpected) move. In the mid-1970s and in mid-problems, they suddenly received notice from the ambitious young landlord to quit their home. They fought back, lost, packed, and left Paris, re-deploying to a small mountain-top in the foothills of the lower Alps. There, in place of the somewhat gruesome view into the bacteriological labs of the university medical school they enjoyed in Paris, they had the full sweep of the Maure mountains, a view that drifted on beyond the Mont Ste Victoire, along to the Luberons and into the Gard: a compensation for their lack of furniture (stuck in the *garde-meuble* until they could find enough money to have it join them) and lack of work (Searle had hardly sat down since New Year's Eve 1969). But Searle's faithful friends Tessa Sayle in London and John Locke in New York – both also his agents – soon solved that one and before long the furniture was out of hock

and the work and the champagne (Searle's engine oil) flowed again.

Now these one-time globe-trotting Parisians are virtually impossible to budge. They revel in the secrecy of their hideout, casual visitors are firmly discouraged and their life is almost conspiratorial in its privacy. Their friends and the locals – mountain people – understand and co-operate. But, like education and intelligence, one should not confuse solitude with isolation. The Searles are not faintly isolated. Living as they do, both on borrowed time, they treat each day as a big slice of cake to be savoured to the final crumb. They have no time for those who leave half a slice on their plate for lack of appetite or interest. Searle's work is probably better than it ever was, and for the last decade he has taken to this cell-like, but totally unmonastic life, like some trout in a mountain stream, steadily moving towards source with every ounce of energy he can muster. Searle, who has been a major influence on succeeding generations of graphic artists in England and America has, in a certain sense, always remained a 'survivor' – a loner, indelibly marked by the slim chance that allowed him to return from one jungle and prepare for the next. He may still sleep with one eye open and his hand at the ready for his pen, but he does so with a lashing of wit, and a touch of offbeat fantasy that has marked him for a long time now as one of the most original humorists of our time, and arguably the finest graphic draughtsman of this century.

Going Back

y friend Vera Volkova once lived in a block of flats by the Liteiny Bridge in Leningrad – the bridge that leads to the Finland Station. I doubt if any of us quite realized the strength of the forces that were dragging her back there.

She began life in the grand manner. For just one year before the Revolution she was one of the *Smolnianki*, little girls who attended Smolny Institute. This school for the daughters of aristocrats had been modelled on Mme de Maintenon's school at St Cyr. Vera got in because her grandfather had been employed at court as a doctor.

Overnight her school became Lenin's HQ – they didn't even have time to take down the notices that said NO TALKING ON THE STAIRS. Vera was moved to 'State School No. 25' and the family were transferred from their balcony flat overlooking the Neva to a servants' room on the courtyard. It was partly to improve family rations that she became a dancer – and it was because she was a dancer that she got the chance to leave Russia in the late 1920s and eventually reach England via China.

I met her in Paris in 1939 when she was going to classes with Egorova and (sometimes) Preobrajenskaya in Montmartre. Over drinks at the bar of the Salle Wacker, a complex of studios in the rue de Douai, she told me about her early days and the people she'd known, such as Shostakovich whom she met through her mother (a musician) when he was playing piano in a cinema. The cinema happened to adjoin Vera's ballet school and was owned by the school's famous director Akim Volynsky, who took a special interest in Vera. (This did her no good at all, especially when he fell out of favour with the authorities.) The atmosphere of those times is well described in Igor Schwezoff's *Borzoi*: the hectic rivalry of the many competing schools, and the passionate love of dance sustained by dancers who were most of the time half starved. Even Volynsky went to bed on winter nights in fur coat, fur cap and galoshes. But Vera spoke most of all about her teachers: the Vaganova whose creative reforms were going to influence ballet throughout the world, and Romanova whose daughter Ulanova was the rising star . . .

When I met her Vera had more or less said goodbye to her own future in ballet. So I was surprised when I returned to London after the war to find her launched on a meteoric new career as international teacher, for which she had to thank Margot Fonteyn, whom she'd known in Shanghai, and Diana Gould, soon to become the wife of Yehudi Menuhin. Vera was now not only coaching Margot in the more difficult roles, but her studio off Cambridge Circus had become a mecca to the foreign troupes then converging on London – which for a moment seemed to have become dance capital of the world.

Her renown was to depend on two things: the card dealt her by fate to communicate Vaganova's teaching to the western world, and her own remarkable gifts of expression which enabled her to pass on that teaching in a vivid way. Wherever dancers are gathered together they still swap stories of Vera and her brilliant use of language in the cause of ballet teaching. The fact that neither English nor French was her native tongue certainly helped: she was able to use both with complete abandon. Vaganova had employed what she called her *vspomogáteli* (helpers), of which an example was 'You don't *do* a step, you *become* it.' Vera developed the idea intriguingly: Pretend (she would say) that you hold between your arms a huge snowball of cottonwool (which on other days might become the whole of Cambridge Circus). Then reach up to grasp the beard of God. Hold your head thus, to smell the violets over your right shoulder. Imagine your fingers have tiny weights on them or (alternatively) tiny lungs growing on the wrists. She would say things like, 'Leg does not know is going to arabesque.' The syntax was wild but it worked. She had immense charm, as well as that inimitably straight Leningrad nose which had made Volynsky cry – in one of his long, boring articles that were not usually reckless in praise – 'Videlyetsya krasivy profily Volkovoy!' She was small and trim, and could look like an urchin or a sophisticated lady according to her mood. It was to everybody's chagrin that she was at last claimed permanently by the Continent, going first to La Scala at Milan and then to the Royal Danish Ballet as artistic adviser. In fact she belonged to the world, travelling far and wide as guest teacher. In the end I only saw her when the plane touched down in London – or when I visited her fiefdom, the Royal Theatre, Copenhagen.

The longer I knew her, the better I came to know Leningrad. Before ever going there I knew the layout of the place, and how to find the flat by Liteiny Bridge. I even knew what Leningrad smelt like: a mix of perfume in the cold air, snow on fur, hot chocolate at the Café des Gourmets. She was nostalgic as only Russians can be – and the only place she could never return to, it seemed, was her home.

Then, ironically, it was I who 'returned'. First I sought out her apartment house. I carefully identified the first-floor flat farthest from the bridge (I had been well briefed) and then visited the courtyard at the back, to guess which of the top maids' rooms had housed (like sardines) the post-Revolutionary Volkovs. I remember sitting in my hotel bedroom, which looked out on St Isaac's Cathedral, describing in a letter all I'd seen. I said it was like a dilapidated palace and she liked the phrase, recognizing herself as that 'urchin from dilapidated palace, wandering, dreaming along the canals'. And she added: 'I don't often allow myself the luxury of opening that secret door'.

She now became more nostalgic than ever to see the place again, but at the same time she was afraid: 'Memories flood my mind and I do not know how to cope with them. Something deep down in me resents the fact that none of my family died a natural death.' Yet it was inevitable that – with her growing celebrity and the relaxing of Soviet rules – she would one day be invited back officially. It happened, and in June 1967 I received a postcard from Leningrad: 'It is a strange dream. Walking for miles everywhere.' Then on 30 August a letter:

How can I explain what I felt, standing in front of my house on the Kutuzov Embankment. My thoughts were as overwhelming and confused as the Neva itself in Spring, when suddenly the ice begins to melt and huge blocks with jagged edges are carried down by the tide with tremendous speed and noise. They push, overtake and pile on top of each other, revealing dark, cold water, while above it all the sun just mocks. As a child, a little frightened and very excited, I watched it from that very house, sitting on my favourite place, the window-sill. To think that I, who checked in at the Astoria Hotel as a tourist, am the same person!

The house, I must say, looks dignified, wonderful proportions, a bit sad. The saddest thing was that nobody's left of my family. My sister Ira just disappeared. I was praying for a miracle – that she might be one of the museum-keepers, and I looked so carefully at their faces, just in case. The city is beautiful and I'm happy I saw it again. I don't regret going back, despite this deep sorrow.

What made me happy, though, was the reception given by the ballet people. As I walked into one classroom the teacher narrowed his eyes and then cried 'Verotchka!' and kissed me. It was Alexander Pushkin, Nureyev's teacher. Then he said: 'Do you remember, Verotchka, when we danced Romances sans paroles *together? Ulanova's mother arranged the choreography.' This was so touching: I was seventeen at the time. I find they know all about me professionally. I was allowed to see all the rehearsals, all the classes. One thing impressed me deeply: how kind everybody is and what good manners they have. I loved meeting them all. They are proud, intelligent, uncomplaining. I felt that their life is hard by ordinary standards, although ballet people enjoy certain privileges. I expect the other thing I'll remember is walking back from the Kirov to the hotel, late at night after the performances – white nights, glittering canals, no traffic, like a stage set for an old Italian opera, with deep shadows and a complete silence.*

In May 1973 Vera was again in Russia, this time with the Royal Danish Ballet. She wrote me her account of it, dated 15 July, while flying back from a professional engagement in Atlanta:

I want to tell you how much I enjoyed that last visit to Russia. I was invited home by all my friends, which would have been unthinkable a few years ago, and it made such a difference. Both lots of directors – from the Bolshoi in Moscow and the Kirov in Leningrad – were really excited to see me, and in some ways I think they were proud of me. In Leningrad there was also a party arranged by the dancers who remembered me, though one or two were out of town and some had died (including Pushkin). We drank Russian champagne (not bad!). It was a real Carnet de Bal atmosphere of warmth and reunion.

Leningrad looked more beautiful than I ever remember it. As my companion I found a young conductor about to sit for his final exams, who loves wandering, and we walked for miles, over the bridges, by the Neva and canals. I hardly slept and just had enough energy to give company class in the morning. I found a house on the way to the Kirov (45 Ulitsa Gertsena) which I just loved. Today it is occupied by the Union of Composers, but it was built by a famous French architect for himself. Small, elegant, mysterious, it was called MY HOUSE. *Late one evening my conductor friend was accompanying me back to the hotel and offered to play me some Sibelius. I wasn't sure the Astoria had a piano – but we found one in a bar. To the astonishment of the tourists with their Scotches, a performance was improvised. The Russian waiter was deeply moved. All this happened about 1 a.m.*

The next day I went to see my own house again. I tried to peep through some holes in the doors of the stables, where my father kept his two horses. The old wood was painted sang de boeuf *and, as I fingered the lock, hoping to find perhaps a saddle or lost ornament, a window opened and a woman cried out: what was I doing there? She came down, very suspicious. I tried to explain that I lived in the house long ago and that what she called 'storage space' used to be stables. After that she invited me to drink tea with her in the basement.*

I am still quite intoxicated by Leningrad. I felt at times that I had never left it. I love the city and I love the people. In Leningrad they have more interesting faces than in Moscow: grave faces, strong eyebrows, straighter noses, better manners. One young girl in a bookshop was so disappointed, when told they didn't have Camus in translation, that her eyebrows just quivered.

I also spent an evening with Ulanova in Moscow and promised to 'look at' the old house in Leningrad (corner of Gogol and Gorohovaya streets) where she lived with her parents and I often went. I kept my promise. I stood in front of the house as one is supposed to do. Everything is still simmering within me. I was so terribly happy there this time. Perhaps after all it is my country . . .

Vera died two years later. Whichever was her country, I think Clement Crisp got it right when he wrote, 'The world is darker, colder without her.'

'Hot Running Water and Paradise Birds'

t was a phrase used of *dachas* to denote impossible luxury and belonged to those days of the late 1960s when queues formed at street corners for speckled apples, and a small bar of Skaska chocolate cost one rouble (£1) in the echoing food halls of Gorky Street. But the non-affluent society had its compensations and one of them was the great ferment of intellectual curiosity that seemed to bubble up everywhere – its purpose, as in wartime London, to combat the greyness and provide some excitement. Foreign literature was then the great escape and, English books being allowed in fairly freely, one got used to meeting girls who had read, for instance, all of Iris Murdoch or who, alternatively, knew great slabs of Salinger by heart. Whether these achievements were really necessary was beside the point: it's the gesture that counts.

Poor in material things, but very eager to grasp spiritual ones, young Russia was in a lively, questing mood. The search for paradise birds was nowhere more marked than in Leningrad at night in the cafés of the Nevsky Prospekt, about which it is impossible not to write affectionately. Among the students at the Sever, for instance, I discussed with a strikingly pretty girl what she called the 'cool humour' of Aldous Huxley, a writer lately rediscovered. The conversation moved on to cool jazz and cool chicks. I had ordered (on her suggestion) a favourite twosome, champagne and black coffee, but already the coffee was cooling and the champagne ignored. She hung, most gratifyingly, on my every word: words like 'Penelope Mortimer'. Yes, soon she would come to London. Last year she had had the choice of two weeks there or two *months* in Georgia. She had plumped for Georgia and did not regret it. It was wonderful. But next time was London's time. Finally she accepted the paperback by John Updike which I was carrying, as if it were some priceless bauble – as indeed it was, J.U. being quite clearly described on the back as 'the new Salinger'.

That was Leningrad. Moscow by comparison was still the big village, a pleasant countrified place of stolid men and women, awash with trees and flowers, in appearance not unlike a Paris suburb or some rambling provincial town of the Midi. Built, you feel, by peasants who did all they could to keep it country. And, to add to the illusion, it had many cosy wooden houses and holes in the pavement.

But Leningrad was so obviously created by a race of urban aristocrats that the two towns are destined forever to be at daggers drawn. Neatly linked by the Red Arrow (400 miles in eight hours) they stand in mutual relation as Paris to Marseilles – always supposing that dear Marseilles has overnight become the capital of France.

Muscovites are kind. One night a group of us blundered into the Maly Theatre during a performance. Up came the manager, smiling, to take us on a conducted tour which ended in our watching the end of the play from a box. I can't think of any theatre in London where this could happen. As a journalist I was invited to meet the personalities of my choice. I chose Richard Aldington's translator Mikhail Urnov and the actress Marina Orlova, who took me to a performance I shall never forget – a morning matinée for one thousand schoolchildren.

Leningraders rather disdain to discuss Moscow, except to laugh a little at the more monstrous confections of the Sovietococo or Wedding Cake style. Muscovites, however, took care to warn us about Leningrad: it was a grey city full of grey people who never smile. Someone from Marseilles might talk like this about Parisians. It is a question, in the end, of temperament.

One can only speak personally. When I got up in Moscow, before breakfast, to go out and discover the Art Theatre, it was a great thrill to find it there on that famous street while, all around, the crowds swarmed on their way to work.

But when I got up in Leningrad to walk along the quays of the Moika (it would be 8.15 and I could smell the tangy canal water) the children were going to school, little girls so elegant in their black-brown dresses, with the red scarves and white aprons; and they gave you, those girls, a long, cool, interested look, and then perhaps a quick smile, not the kind a Muscovite might notice, but you felt somehow admitted to their city.

Leningrad today does not seem like a place of horror, where 632,000 people starved to death. It does not even seem like the birthplace of revolution. It has gone back to being the most romantic town in the world, where Canaletto riverscapes alternate with dark, quiet canals, and students on the Nevsky are still more than a little in love with foreign literature while waiting for *glasnost*.

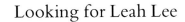

Looking for Leah Lee

The poet Jules Laforgue had been four years in Berlin as French Reader to the Empress Augusta when he met the English girl Leah Lee. In that January of 1886, when he first took English lessons from her, he was 25 years old.

Later that year, on 6 September, he proposed – and they were married in Addison Road, London W14, on 31 December. A few months later Laforgue died in Paris of tuberculosis (1887) while Leah died of the same disease the following year.

The questions I had to answer were: who was she and where did she come from?

Leah is first revealed to us in Laforgue's letter to his friends the Ysaÿes when he says: 'Did I tell you that I'm marvellously in love with a young English girl, my professor of English, and that I might well become engaged? It would be a beautiful and positive act. What adorable novels I'd write then!' The girl was living alone in Berlin, studying painting and giving English lessons. Though fragile in appearance she was headstrong enough to have stormed out of the family home when her father, left a widower, married the governess. In looks she was striking, having red hair, a milky complexion and big dark eyes: she conformed to Laforgue's ideal. There were three sexes, he said: men, women and English girls; and, if he could choose, he would pick a thin English schoolteacher. Miss Lee was slender enough to satisfy his most exacting requirements. As the Tuesday and Saturday lessons proceeded in her lodgings at 57 Königrätzerstrasse he began to confide in his other friends, first with Gustave Kahn: 'You can't imagine the sort of life I'm leading this winter. I've been going to a series of balls, and I talk for hours with beings who are absolutely strange to me: young girls' – and he mentions one in particular: 'an absurd and astonishing little person who is English.' By the end of the summer he was planning marriage and writing to his sister: 'Her name is pronounced "Lia Li" in French. She's a funny little thing impossible to describe. I call her Petit Personnage.' The letter is important because it contains most of the available clues to her identity.

She has many sisters and brothers, the letter says. One of the brothers is a lawyer in Folkestone, another is a priest in New Zealand and a third is an officer in Zululand. She has one 'favourite' brother, but the letter does not indicate which one it is. Her mother died four years before, and her father remarried against the wishes of his children, who left him. Leah went to a boarding school in Switzerland, where she learnt to speak excellent French, and then to Berlin where she had been for the last two years, living off her English lessons, with a small allowance from her father. She was a protestant but not very religious. She had no dowry.

There was not much more to go on, except that in the marriage register of St Barnabas Church, Addison Road, she described her father as 'Samuel Lee, Gentleman' and gave her age as 22. That meant she was born in 1864, and anyone looking her up under that year at Somerset House, would find that she did not exist. Most of these few facts revealed themselves to be so doubtful and contradictory that a previous researcher had decided that she was a blacksmith's daughter from Erith who had made the whole lot up in order to sound more interesting.

I turned to someone who had actually known her, Laforgue's friend Gustave Kahn, who claimed to recognize her in two heroines of Laforgue's *Moral Tales*. Kahn says unequivocally in more than one article that she was the Andromède of 'Persée et Andromède', as well as the Syrinx of 'Pan et la Syrinx'. He saw in these characters not only her 'svelte allure' and 'grace profonde' but instanced particular passages, such as Andromède's· fits of impatience and Syrinx's cool composure, which expressed different facets of Leah's own temperament.

Little Andromède is as capricious as she is charming. She has red hair, thick and silky, which – when she puts it up – tends to be too top-heavy for her tiny face and long neck. She conforms perfectly to the Laforguian canon, having small breasts, slim straight hips and legs that are 'strangely long and fine'. Her eyes can be wan and dim, or clear as a seagull's. Laforgue refers specifically to her black seagull's eyes. (In a poem of the same year he also calls them 'coffee eyes'.) At times Andromède has a slightly ravaged look (which reminds one of a Laforguian fragment saying: 'She was very young, with the face of a baby which on certain days could look very tired. On those days, if she told me a lie – smiling, with her eyes wide open, looking at me directly – that tired face suddenly freshened as if kissed by the breezes of her native land)'.

Likewise in the Syrinx Kahn recognized only too well the ardent and pale countenance of that nymph, who was at once wilful, rebellious and proud, naïvely proud with a thousand susceptibilities. Kahn had often seen those sad cheeks beneath the big eyes which could be both surprised and determined. Twice he uses the word 'determined' ('décidé'). Leah and the Syrinx were high-spirited and witty girls who were also impatient, wilful, rebellious, complicated and determined. And Syrinx seems even to speak like Leah when she asks: 'Vraiment? . . . Mais quoi? . . .' And when she says, 'Je ne suis pas un petit paon' one can clearly hear Leah saying, 'Je ne suis pas un petit personnage'.

Somerset House might say she didn't exist, but for me she was very real. To back a hunch I began with some fairly basic research about the Laforgues' weekend in London at the end of 1886. And what a weekend for a wedding that was! In the preceding autumn they had left Berlin separately – Laforgue for Paris, Leah for England – with the plan that Leah would join him in Paris. Instead of which Laforgue comes to England, and some of his friends will maintain ever afterwards that it killed him. The weather, as described in *The Times*, could hardly have been worse: there was snow and ice, freezing fog and a gale. But I found at the Guildhall the marriage affidavit I was looking for.

When they returned to Paris things went from bad to worse. Laforgue fell ill almost at once and wrote: 'Luckily the petit personnage I married has a skinny kid's good health – I'm looked after with fun and fantasy.' In April he says that 'Li' (sic)⋆ is funnier than ever with hair cropped short. ('Elle est très drôle avec ses cheveux coupés presque ras.') In May: 'She's such a funny little character – I'm looked after with a happy smile and big eyes.' Leah's own health must have been

⋆The actor Jean-Louis Barrault has made the intriguing suggestion that, when Laforgue's Hamlet (in *Moral Tales*) calls his Ophélie 'Lili' for short, 'Lili' could equally well be spelt 'Lee-Lee'.

worsening but it is never mentioned: was he too ill to notice, or did she deceive him too well with her fun and fantasy? Laforgue died at 6 a.m. on the morning of 20 August. And so to that pathetic funeral: the cemetery worker waving a wooden cross and shouting to the mourners, 'Are you lot for Laforgue?' – followed by Leah's desperate little laugh . . .

According to all the accounts Leah made one final appearance before retiring to Menton to die: it was to hand over a suitcase, containing all her husband's manuscripts, to his friend Teodor de Wyzewa in Paris. Pascal Pia has saluted her for destroying nothing – 'Not the palest pencil scrawl on the smallest scrap of paper' – and recommended it to all authors' widows.

But again who was she?

Her handwriting, as revealed on marriage register and affidavit, was that of a typical English schoolgirl. The words 'Leah Lee' in round English script suggested neither Andromède nor the Syrinx but I was determined to find the girl behind them. So I returned to Somerset House, where the departments of Births, Marriages and Deaths were then maintained. I worked conscientiously but it was not a place conducive to the unravelling of family tangles: too much competition from the clerks of law offices hurling the heavy tomes about with lethal effect. When the going got tough I used to retire to Wills, a quieter enclave across the vast courtyard, and it may have been there that I made the first break-through, leading to the conviction that Leah was a Devon girl, the daughter of a prosperous Teignmouth draper. From now on the word 'Teignmouth' was engraved on my heart (and visited my dreams). Yet it was still remote from that other word 'Laforgue': none of the endless permutations between births, deaths, marriages and wills ever included Laforgue.

A time of great frustration now began, when my obsessions grew to absurd proportions: they became what Richard Holmes in *Footsteps* has called 'a haunting . . . an encroachment of the present upon the past and, in some sense, of the past upon the present.' I probably went a bit mad, as Holmes did in his pursuit of Gérard de Nerval, an adventure which ended, you may remember, with his falling through the skylight of a roof in Paris. I searched for Leah in Menton and surrounding villages but without success: no grave, no death certificate. I was seized with a sudden desire to possess the original of her only recorded letter, which had been written to Wyzewa when she handed over the papers. Wyzewa had given it to G. Jean-Aubry who in his turn had died. His widow had remarried, then divorced and disappeared. (But I found that letter and have it still.) In my diary of those troubled times I see that in the spring of 1964 I wrote to the *Teignmouth Post*, who printed my letter on 1 May. The readers of that modest journal must have been fairly surprised to read (if any of them did) my heartfelt plea for news of Leah, with a detailed account of all my proud discoveries to date. There was no reply. I next turned my attention to *Books*, the journal of the National Book League, but this time decided to keep my discoveries to myself. *Books* agreed to print my appeal but not before their issue of Jan-Feb 1965. More nail-biting but in the end the wait was worth it: early in March a letter dropped through my letter-box from a Mrs Sybil Marshall (how I blessed that name!). Her daughter had married the great-nephew of Leah Laforgue. And when the great-nephew himself (Anthony Atmore) brought family photographs to my flat on 23 March, I was thrilled to see on the backs of all of them the magic word TEIGNMOUTH. The connection had been made. The chase was ended.

At the same time Tony Atmore told me of a traditional belief in the family that Leah had died in England. Up till then I had meekly accepted the Menton version, but when I returned to Somerset House, there she was: she'd been there all the time, albeit misspelt 'Laforge'. I found she had died at a Kilburn convent on 6 June 1888, having arrived there from Menton's 'House for Consumption' (sic).

There now only remained the question: where was she buried? In London presumably, though Bedford was possible, for that is where the Lees were living in 1888, having moved there from Teignmouth in 1884. I suppose I had traipsed round most of the London cemeteries – and was preparing wearily to entrain for Bedford – when it suddenly occurred to me that the family could still have chosen Teignmouth, since that was where the mother would have been buried in 1883. Consulting my diary once more I find that on 28 April the Verger of St James's Church, Teignmouth, wrote to confirm that Leah Laforge (sic) and her mother were buried side by side at Teignmouth and that, in the case of the former, the funeral was conducted by 'the Priest in charge of Skye'. A day or two later the Cemetery foreman gave me the actual location and on 7 May I travelled down. My supreme moment came the following day when, in the hilltop graveyard, I pulled back the branch of an overhanging tree to reveal the name LEAH LAFORGUE.

Back in London Tony Atmore brought along to our next meeting (11 May) another of Leah's great-nephews, the Rev Clive Warwick Lee. I showed them the photographs I had taken of Leah's tomb and the Lee family house at Teignmouth. With their considerable help, and that of local newspapers found at the British Museum Newspaper Library, Colindale, I was able to write the full-page article that established Leah's identity in the *Times Literary Supplement* of 10 June 1965. Clive Lee wrote the fuller official account, 'Leah Laforgue, her parents and family' for Warren Ramsey's *Jules Laforgue: Essays on a poet's life and work* (Southern Illinois University Press, 1969).

Leah Lee was born at Teignmouth, Devon, on 9 April, 1861. She was thus only eight months younger than Laforgue – and not three years as stated incorrectly in the marriage register. Of Devon stock on both sides (mostly sailors and farmers) she was one of the sixteen children of Samuel Lee and his wife Leah (née Page), who married in 1853. Three of the children died in infancy and those surviving were (in chronological order): Fanny, Edgar, Lewis, Herbert, Leah, Ernest, Kate, Edith, Bertha, Ethel, Arthur, Warwick and Percival.

Samuel was the leading draper of Teignmouth. It was he who brought the latest fashions to this seaside town. After a few years in partnership he launched out on his own in 1856 and continued for 25 years on the same site in Regent Street, Teignmouth, later occupied by Radford's. He was able to retire in his early fifties, and died in 1895 aged 68. 'Sammy' Lee was long remembered in these parts as a wide-awake businessman. Indeed all the Lees were able and active. One of the sons, Ernest Page Lee (1862-1932) was a barrister who became New Zealand's Minister of Justice in the Massey Cabinet during the First World War.

Leah's 'favourite' brother turns out to have been Edgar, who was four years her senior and a High Anglican priest. He was a spirited man who liked good living and moved about in an aura of controversy. Indeed 'Father' Lee finally left the Church of England altogether to become a Roman Catholic. Besides a strong and forceful character he had exceptional musical gifts. When Laforgue in the letter to his sister refers to Leah's brothers, including 'the lawyer at Folkestone and the priest in New Zealand', he got his signals crossed. It should have been the other way round: the priest (Edgar) at Folkestone, the lawyer (Ernest) in New Zealand. His slip of the pen, like the mistake over Leah's age in the marriage register, led to total confusion among scholars.

Leah was educated in Teignmouth and at the Maynard School, Exeter. Teignmouth was always a good place for children to grow up in: there was such a choice of exciting things to do. As well as the sea, there was the harbour and the river and, on the other side of the river, the sweeping hills of Haldon Moor and the great red cliff called The Ness. Not only are the cliffs and rocks red in this part of Devon. Even the sand on Teignmouth beach is red; and everywhere in the town you hear the sea and the sea-gulls. It was an ideal setting for little Andromède – though Laforgue never knew Teignmouth, any more than Leah knew Laforgue's own native town of Tarbes.

Since Teignmouth was a port, some of Samuel's merchandise must have arrived by sea, and I was delighted to find an advertisement placed in the press by Laforgue's future father-in-law – for Paris-wove corsets. Is it possible that Leah stayed with the supplier of those corsets when she first visited Paris (Asnières to be precise) in 1878?

Samuel rose quickly to become a pillar of local society. Already in 1863, for the wedding celebrations of the Prince of Wales and Princess Alexandra, the 'imposing decorations' of S. Lee's store were much remarked on: there were 'three columns of evergreens interspersed with flags, with the royal initials formed of leaves and flowers.' He was also on the committee of the big ball held in the Assembly Rooms, those magnificent Assembly Rooms which, flanked by the twin wings of Den Crescent, remained the architectural hub of Teignmouth, even when metamorphosed later as the Riviera Cinema.

Samuel was a typical Victorian, a stout and sometimes wrathful man, sharply enterprising but honest. He would stand stolidly, watch in hand at 8 a.m., as his staff arrived for work. Even his children had to make appointments to see him. When he retired in 1881 he became a 'Gentleman' with a coat-of-arms. The family then moved from 7-8 Regent Street (over the shop) to 'Rosenville', the last house at the east end (north side) of Bank Street.

It was in this house that Leah's mother died in September 1883 – and not 1884 as Laforgue had implied in the letter to his sister. The death was a terrible blow to Samuel. For one thing she had always been his very active personal assistant, even travelling as a buyer on the Continent in the intervals between her sixteen confinements. But most of all he was affected emotionally, becoming for a time almost demented. Though most of the shops closed as a mark of respect on the day of the funeral, Samuel himself was nowhere to be seen. Most uncharacteristically he had thrown up his hands in despair, making no attempt to bury the dead woman . . .

An anecdote remembered in the family is that Bertha's

14th birthday occurred as the mother was dying, and was consequently overlooked until Leah took off her own favourite bracelet to give to her young sister. Also at this time another sister, Ethel, aged 11 (grandmother of Tony Atmore) was packed off alone to join her brother Ernest in New Zealand and, since the voyage would take eight weeks, it was Leah again who made up for the girl eight little parcels, each containing a change of clothes.

Nine months after the death of his wife, Samuel Lee, now 57, married the children's governess, Louisa Crawford (37) and left Teignmouth for Bedford with all the younger children. (They were to stay there for the next four years before returning west again to Exmouth.) Leah and the older children became estranged from their father because of his supposedly 'unsuitable' marriage to 'Auntie Lou'. Leah, who had already started school in Switzerland for her French, now switched to Berlin for her German. Clive Lee suggests that she found some sort of job at the Court but this is uncertain.

During the three months that Leah waited in England, prior to her marriage at the end of 1886, it is doubtful if relations between father and daughter much improved. Leah was probably too proud to involve him in her affairs. With Edgar, however, who was now 29 and a curate at Folkestone, things were very different. They must have seen a lot of each other that autumn. No doubt it was Edgar too who arranged the church for her wedding as well as temporary accommodation for her in the lodgings of the St Barnabas junior curate. She would also have seen something of her sister Kate (22) who had become a nun in a Church of England convent at East Grinstead. It seems that both Edgar and Kate had been influenced in their religious vocations by a local church they had attended at Shaldon, across the river from Teignmouth.

We now know that Leah wrote to Laforgue every day (in English) during those three months spent waiting for the wedding. If the letters have vanished, it is possibly because Leah herself destroyed them. Her respect for anything that might be called a literary manuscript did not apparently extend to letters.

On the day of Laforgue's death she immediately sent a telegram to Kate in the convent. The nuns' records (examined by Clive Lee) are so exact that we know the actual train Kate caught: the 4.06 to Victoria which connected with the 8 p.m. boat train, which meant she arrived in Paris at 5.05 on Sunday morning. It is good to know that Leah had some support, though Kate had leave only till Wednesday.

Leah was now seriously ill. The so-called 'House for Consumption' to which she was admitted at Menton was in reality the Villa Helvetia, a small nursing home for women situated among olive groves above the Bay of Garavan to the east of the town. While there she sent a small picture of herself to little Bertha, now 18. St Peter's Convent, where she died, is a building that no longer exists, destroyed by a flying bomb on 29 June 1944.

After her death Leah's body was taken by train to the Teignmouth she had known as a child. The faithful Edgar, now the priest in charge of St Columba's Mission, Isle of Skye, made the long journey from the north of Scotland to the south of Devon to take his favourite sister's funeral.

From St James's Church, with its 13th century tower of red sandstone, the procession struggled slowly up the Exeter road, a one-in-ten gradient between red walls, to the little *cimetière marin* on the hill.

Here lies Leah, buried beside her parents at the foot of a cypress tree where in spring the ground is covered with wild violets and primroses. At the base of a white stone cross the inscription reads:

LEAH LAFORGUE
daughter of Samuel and Leah Lee
died June 6th 1888
aged 27 years
'Jesu, Mercy'

If her name is at last spelt correctly, it will have been due to faithful Edgar.

On publication of my book *Looking for Laforgue* (Carcanet, 1979) I received a letter from George D. Painter, the biographer of Proust: 'Teignmouth! I spent two Junes there aged nine and ten, roaming the dark streets, the luminous sands, the waterfront from the harbour along the sea wall to Smugglers' Lane, from which Leah was already gone, and now you have brought her back, ailing but still in her twenties. How touching it is, how mysterious! . . . Your identification of poor Leah Lee is one of the great discoveries of our time.'

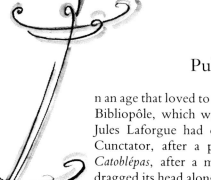

Publisher of Poets

n an age that loved to invent new words he was known as the
Bibliopôle, which was a Greek way of saying Bookseller.
Jules Laforgue had other names for him such as Fabius
Cunctator, after a procrastinating Roman emperor, and
Catoblépas, after a mythical, long-necked monster which
dragged its head along the ground. Authors generally (in the
way of authors) called him mean and dilatory; critics
criticized his publicity methods which they considered infra
dig for a serious publisher (more reminiscent of department
stores, they said). But a serious publisher he was, for did not
his list include Verlaine, Moréas and Laforgue? And in his
prime Léon Vanier became known as Father of the Decadents
and Publisher of the Moderns.

The man was revealed in all his splendour in Jean-Louis
Debauve's *Laforgue en son temps* (1972). Debauve is a Paris
judge and his uncle Charles Martyne was a man about
literary Paris at the turn of the century; like all young men of
the period he was mad about Laforgue. One such young
man, Paul Adam, had gone so far as to place Laforgue as the
last link in the chain: Moses, Aeschylus, Virgil, Dante,
Rabelais, Shakespeare, Goethe, Flaubert, Laforgue. The
twenty-three-year-old Monsieur Martyne did not go that far
but on 25 April 1899 he went as far as Vanier's shop and
bought the Laforgue dossier from him for 130 frs. including
correspondence, cuttings and proofs. To give some idea of
contemporary values: Laforgue used to pay 100 frs. for a
good suit from Cossard's on the boulevard des Italiens (and
it was a good deal more than he could afford). Thanks to M.
Martyne's dossier it is now possible to examine the relations
between a poet and his publisher in the 1880s and to consider
them perhaps as a paradigm of all such relationships.

It began in January 1884. Vanier had been established for
six years as publisher-bookseller at 19 quai Saint-Michel.
Laforgue, who was French Reader at the Berlin Court, was
casting around for a publisher for his first book *Les Complaintes*. To his friend Charles Henry in Paris he wrote on 8
January, 'Have you received my *Complaintes*? Could you
deal with them, when you have a moment, in the way you
think best? I'll pay of course – but let's publish quickly and
get it over with. Any chance, do you think, of their appearing in April?'

It went without saying that poets in those days paid to be
published. The only exception in Vanier's list was Verlaine
himself and even he had paid for his masterpiece *Sagesse*. So
the poets contributed in varying degrees to the costs and
shared likewise in the net profits. On receipt of Laforgue's
letter Henry got a quotation from the well-known firm of
Alphonse Lemerre; but Laforgue on 20 January was not
satisfied:

*Oh my poor book, I find the bill terrifying! Let me explain that for
a whole lot of reasons I am living at the moment on my next
quarter's salary [April-June] and I shan't be able to offer 700 frs. to
any printer before 1st January next year, the most I could possibly
give on account being 300 frs. in July. But in any case do we really
need a de luxe job on laid paper? Wouldn't it be better to apply to
that ideal Léon Vanier on the quayside just before you get to
Notre-Dame, who prints the poems of Verlaine, Valade, etc. on*

divine grocer's paper. We'd order an edition with the smallest number of copies possible, third class as with funerals, and we'd give him 300 frs. in July. Lemerre must surely be drunk with the success of his gift books with colour illustrations for him to take such a 'famillionaire' tone with a poor rhymer like me!

And on 13 March he wrote to Charles Henry again:

Thanks for all your trouble with the book . . . I've just written to Vanier, who must be intelligent to have published Paris moderne, *including Verlaine after his troubles. I'm saying the MS is complete. I'll pay him 200 frs. in July and I've asked him for all the details about format and extra copies (and told him to send the proofs to me, which should be sufficient).*

Paris moderne was a periodical that Vanier had published briefly in 1882-3. It was printed on what seemed like white packing paper and featured the poems of Verlaine's *Jadis et Naguère* that Vanier was to publish as a book in 1884. Laforgue's note to Vanier had said:

I agree with your conditions (which M. Henry has forwarded to me) for publishing my book of poems. A print of 500 and we share the profits, for which publication (once we've fixed the details) I promise to pay you 200 frs. on 1st July 1884. The MS is complete and I'd like the printing to start as soon as possible – the proofs to be sent me (either section by section or altogether) at the following address: the Palace of the Princesses, Berlin, until 20 April, and then : Hôtel Messmer, Baden-Baden.

It later transpired that the cost of printing alone (excluding paper) was 360 frs., to which Laforgue contributed his 200 frs. In the event the 500 copies at 3 frs. each took ten years to sell, but by that time Laforgue was dead. During the next two or three months there couldn't have been much progress because on 23 May he wrote to Henry: 'So you've constituted yourself the guardian angel of my *Complaintes* and I'll get proofs here (Baden-Baden). Provided that the delights of the countryside don't make Vanier forget it altogether.' Two days later Laforgue wrote to Vanier:

My friend M. Henry sent me a note about the book and your decision to get it out as soon as possible in June. That's excellent. Can I count on it? Here is the title page and dedication, which make the thing complete. I look forward to receiving the proofs, which I certainly won't overload with corrections.

Two months later – in mid-July – he sent a note to Henry: 'Vanier is right to wait, and in the meantime I'll be able to make some revisions.' So Vanier was waiting and Laforgue was putting a bright face on it. But why was Vanier waiting? Is it possible that M. Laforgue had omitted to send him his 200 frs. on 1 July and M. Vanier was waiting for his money? Laforgue was notoriously extravagant and what we do know is that a little later he signed two promissory notes of 100 frs. each, payable to M. Vanier in January and April 1885. It seems certain that these were instead of (and not as well as) the 200 frs. originally payable on 1 July 1884. So Vanier was stalling and it is permissible to guess that the poet's annual stay in Paris was marred that year by some bad attacks of the well-known complaint 'author's anxiety'. On the eve of his return to Germany, he sent Vanier a postcard dated 30

October 1884: 'Allow me to remind you with anguish that from 4 November I shall no longer be in Paris.' And this was followed by an even more poignant message on 5 November. Composed in the third person, its writing and spelling suggest that he was probably drunk at the time – either that or hopping mad: 'M. Laforgue leaves the day after tomorrow and begs M. Vannier (*sic*) to send the proofs when they are ready to: M. Henry at 22 rue Berthollet, and a second set to M. Laforgue at the Château, Coblenz, till 1st December.'

So Laforgue returned to Coblenz and waited for the proofs which still didn't arrive. On 28 November he informed Vanier:

This is to inform you, or rather to remind you, that I am leaving Coblenz and from Monday next shall be at the Palace of the Princesses, Berlin. What of the proofs of my Complaintes? *I hope that now I've left Paris and France you won't consider me as distant, lost and mythical and therefore indefinitely negligible. I shall go on waiting with the same impatience.*

It was then that Vanier bestirred himself. At least that is how it must have appeared to Laforgue but perhaps there were mitigating circumstances. We now have to introduce the figure of Vanier's printer, Léo Trézenik, with whom he was closely associated and who also happened to be the editor of the literary review *Lutèce* (the Romans' name for Paris) which had a circulation of one thousand. The bookseller-publisher and printer-editor formed a tightly knit team, the bookshop and the printing works being only half a mile from each other in the famous 5th arrondissement. In making his plans Vanier had always to consider the situation at 16 boulevard Saint-Germain (the printing works) – and nearly always it was chaotic. To begin with, Trézenik was chronically short of type – but, this being the reason his charges were low, Vanier could hardly complain. On top of that, however, he had a temperamental urge to take on more than he could cope with. This year in particular he had a heavy workload. In the last four months of 1883 *Lutèce* had printed Verlaine's *Les Poètes Maudits*, an epoch-making series which introduced in persuasive prose the genius of Corbière, Rimbaud and Mallarmé. Then during the first four months of 1884, it was turned into a book, printed by Trézenik and published by Vanier. Later in the year it was the turn of Verlaine the poet, whose *Jadis et Naguère* was closely preceded by Moréas's *Les Syrtes*. So it was only now perhaps that Vanier could decently saddle his printer with Laforgue's *Complaintes*. In any case the next letter in the dossier is from Trézenik to Vanier in December:

For the Complaintes *book, with a print of 520 (sic), the agreed price for each eight-page section shall be 20 frs. and no discount. I shall need four and a half reams of double crown and I prefer to cut it myself so that all the sheets are exactly the same size, which wasn't the case for* Jadis et Naguère. *Please expedite the return of proofs to the best of your ability since there is more composition per page than in the Verlaine. I shall only be able to give you two eight-page sections at a time and until these are printed I shall not be able to proceed with the composition of the next section.*

The last sentence is vital for the understanding of what was to happen. Trézenik had just enough type to set sixteen pages of the *Complaintes*. After he had set them and Laforgue had passed them it was necessary to print them at once so that the type could be distributed and freed for composing the next sixteen pages. This operation had to be repeated nine times, allowing an average of three weeks each time for setting, proofing and printing. Thus the printing period for a relatively slim volume of 144 pages plus cover added up to seven months; and as the tortuous operation proceeded from December 1884 to July 1885 Laforgue seems to have been quite oblivious to the bizarre nature of the enterprise. Indeed Vanier's greatest crime may have been not to put the poet in the picture a little more – it would have helped him to understand. As it was Laforgue knew nothing. He had just about heard of a printer called Trézenik but initially he does not seem to have known he was working for Vanier or that the same Trézenik was the editor of *Lutèce*. He did not therefore know that when Vanier published a book Trézenik gave it free publicity by quoting great chunks of it in *Lutèce* (and thereby acquiring free copy for himself). *Lutèce* (editor Trézenik) could also be used for extolling the virtues of Trézenik, printer. In a rather similar fashion Vanier got free advertisements in various periodicals throughout France in exchange for putting them on sale in his shop. No money changed hands but in a do-it-yourself sort of way the publicity side was well taken care of.

On 16 December Laforgue was still complaining to his friend Gustave Kahn: 'I've written nothing since the *Complaintes*. The idea that Vanier should make a fool of me like this, while the promissory notes I gave him circulate merrily, is something that makes me rage. I'll never present that gentleman with a bunch of roses.' And later the same month there was the anguished cry: 'And Vanier for God's sake?' But in the middle of January out of the blue came some proofs. Laforgue now began wasting time on his own account, taking exception to Vanier's trademark, a sort of female athlete in tights who disported herself on an open book bearing the letters LV. To Kahn on 18 January he wrote: 'I absolutely agree we've got to remove this little prancer of an ex-libris, but Vanier will probably prefer to demolish his shop rather than let her go.' And to Vanier three days later he wrote: 'We shall obviously have to remove the little prancer but what can we put in her place?' Whereupon Vanier made some sort of protest and Laforgue replied firmly (27 January): 'The little prancer (which is not my own name for her) is very sweet but would be quite out of place in the circumstances. I'm awaiting more proofs from day to day. What a long time it takes to publish a volume of poetry!'

The long wait continued. The letters for February are missing but there is quite a spate of them for March. To Kahn on the second he wrote: 'I received your letter at the same time as a second little packet of proofs from Vanier, a chap whose name doesn't even lend itself to a decent pun.' The same day he wrote to Vanier:

At last a few proofs. If the rest of them dribble through at this rate, when will the book appear? Do you realize that I'm leaving Berlin on 1st April to bury myself in Baden-Baden and similar spots? And I can't be published in the summer because none of my friends will be around . . . it would be a disaster. To think that you spoke seriously of bringing me out last December! Oh well, may thy will be done! . . . but let me say once again, Dear M. Vanier, do get a move on

or I shall end up by losing all faith in my offspring and doubting my true paternity.

On 11 March he asked M. Vanier a simple question: 'If I could get you with your back to the wall, what publication date would you promise me?' And on the same day he wrote to Henry: 'If Vanier goes on delaying publication we may as well drop the whole idea. . . . The people who might have bought my book won't be around after 1st May. But all complaints are pointless. May his will be done, and not mine!' Writing to Kahn on 19 March he sounded even more pathetic:

You ask me for some verses. I haven't lined up the least couplet since placing my Complaintes *in the hands of the disappointing Vanier . . . What is he doing, the brute? I'm beginning to find him really too much. And he had the nerve to assure me without blinking that my book would be out last December. If he goes on stalling I'll be sick of the thing even before it's out. . . . If you happen to bump into him, just tell him I'm seething, will you.*

At this point Trézenik began to print the poems in *Lutèce* – he printed seven in five issues – and Laforgue was completely baffled. Not entirely displeased, merely confused. How could it have happened? And when a reader wrote in complaining about the poems' obscurity the editor replied that *Lutèce* was prepared to print anything outrageous whether it was good or bad. Yet twice in letters to Kahn at this time Laforgue spoke well of Trézenik, saying that for his next book he would go directly to 'some civilized printer like Trézenik' and cut out publishers altogether. He was obviously still in the dark.

To Vanier on 13 April he said: 'There are plenty of people of good will around who doubt if my book will ever appear.' And on 23 April: 'I have nothing further to say about the unaccountable slowness of this book's composition. I have given up counting on anything at all.' To Kahn the same day he wrote:

That Catoblépas of a Vanier has sent me a few more proofs. Has he ever spoken to you a bit frankly about the extent to which my book enters (or doesn't enter) into his plans? Do you think he intends to publish it perhaps soon, now that he's encashed my promissory notes? What a gang they are, those publishers!

On 1 May he moaned to Henry: 'Have you any idea what is happening in those higher spheres of publishing administration situated in Vanier's brain? Did he perchance ever mention a date to you for the despatch of the volume?' And later the same month, also to Henry:

I won't say a word about my Complaintes. *You know as much and as little as I do about that lamentable affair. Vanier shall henceforth be given the name Fabius Cunctator – on the basis that if a poet called Cunct entrusts to him a paid up manuscript, then Cunct a tort [is wrong] if he expects it to be turned into a book on an appointed date. The direness of the pun is symptomatic of my morale.*

And now, by sheer bad luck (for Laforgue) one of Vanier's titles went out of print in a single month and since this was such a rare occurrence he had no choice but to tell Trézenik to drop everything and reprint their one and only bestseller. To add insult to injury the book in question was a clever spoof of all so-called decadent modern poetry. It was called *Les Déliquescences d'Adoré Floupette* which might be translated as *The Liquifactions of Vaguefart the Beloved,* and was the work of a couple of enterprising journalists. When *Les Complaintes de Jules Laforgue* finally appeared some readers found them even more bizarre than the spoof. One critic indeed pretended to take Laforgue's work for a spoof and, as such, he pronounced it less amusing than Floupette's.

There was a note of final desperation in Laforgue's message to Vanier of 7 June: 'Your proofs are getting even rarer, but at least you have given me proof of what to expect.' As publication day at last approached Laforgue was like a cat on hot bricks: 'I wait from hour to hour,' he told Vanier on 18 July – and on 23 July: 'At last but alas!' and he proceeded to list the misprints (many of which he had passed himself). Anyone knowing the resources of M. Trézenik would not have been surprised to find him reduced to putting Jeux for Yeux and using grave accents when he ran out of circumflexes. And when one considers the load of corrections on some of Laforgue's 'passed' pages, it is almost surprising he did as well as he did. But to Henry on 26 July Laforgue wrote: 'You'll have had the *Complaintes* by now and you'll have seen the misprints and other mistakes.' And to Kahn on 6 August: 'Vanier kept me guessing till the very last day. Finally it appeared on 25 July. . . . I'm sending you a copy and you'll see that my Moon book is announced on the back. This time Vanier is going to give me proofs all in one go. Says he!' The astonishing news was confirmed to Vanier on 10 August: 'You have my *L'Imitation de la Lune* [sic]. It isn't a big book. . . . So is it agreed? Will you deal with it in a soldierly fashion in 28 days?' In spite of all his

groans Laforgue had decided to place his new book in the hands of his wicked old publisher! Vanier in his youth had written a humorous book called *Les 28 jours d'un réserviste.* Perhaps he enjoyed Laforgue's allusion to it. In any case, unpredictable as ever, he rose to the bait and brought out *L'Imitation de Notre-Dame la Lune* exactly three months later on 12 November. This time Laforgue paid only 100 frs. towards the cost, but it was a slimmer book . . . and then Trézenik needed the work.

Vanier in some ways was one of the first modern publishers, and got little thanks for it. He was a jovial man and his shop a most pleasant literary salon. Dark, small and restless he had a habit of rubbing his hands together with glee as if he had just heard wonderful news. Unkind tongues suggested it was the news of another big sucker landed, but even his enemies never suggested that he had made much of a killing out of publishing. On the contrary he had to go carefully because he was in no way a rich man. His kindness to Verlaine was noticed as well as Verlaine's ingratitude. After Vanier had doled out pocket money to him, Verlaine would reply by calling him an old fishmonger – on the strength of his having once published an article on fly-fishing. And when the cash was no longer forthcoming Verlaine had even been seen to pick up one of his own titles in the shop, take it across the road and sell it at one of the book-boxes along the quays. So Vanier, too, had his troubles.

And if the methods of Léon Vanier are finally considered to have been reprehensible, then it must be admitted that Jules Laforgue soon caught up with them. Two of the best reviews ever to appear of *Les Complaintes* were written by Laforgue himself.

The Tigers' Lair

One of the most famous flats in modern literature was always '69 Clovelly Mansions', where Katherine Mansfield and John Middleton Murry lived together for four hectic months in 1912, and where Katherine had a charlady named Mrs Bates, afterwards immortalized as 'Ma Parker'. But as there are no Clovelly Mansions in the Gray's Inn Road today it was always assumed that the flat had been swept away – possibly at the same time as the trams, which in those days sailed down the famous thoroughfare.

After long perusal of the old Rate Books, however, I discovered that the flat of the Two Tigers, as they were called – alias Wig and Bogey, alias Mansfield and Murry – does still exist but under a different name and number. At about the time of the First World War, 69 Clovelly Mansions became quite simply 19 Churston Mansions. Recently the occupants allowed us to explore the premises and there remains no doubt at all that this was the flat where Mansfield invited Murry to live with her and where they eventually became not only lovers but co-editors of the *avant-garde* review, *Rhythm*.

A pleasant flat built in 1895, it comprised two front rooms, which Katherine called the Writing Room and the Music Room, and behind them, bedroom, bathroom, hall and kitchen. Murry first visited the place in the early spring of 1912. After climbing the steep flights – for in those days Churston Mansions had no lift – he was received in the Writing Room, where he was surprised to find the walls papered with brown packing paper and the floor covered with yellow Japanese matting. Three windows gave on to Gray's Inn Road but there was hardly any furniture. Tea was served in bowls on the floor and there were cushions to sit on.

A day or two later, when he arrived to take her out, she paused as if remembering something and said: 'You haven't really seen my flat. You haven't seen my kitchen, for instance.' Pushing up the window, 'That's my view,' she said. It looked out east towards the City over a vast forest of chimney-pots, with here and there in the distance a tall grey church spire, almost silvery in the sunlight. 'Do you like my view?' she asked. Then she showed him the smaller of the front rooms, the Music Room, which was also called the Buddha Room, after a stone Buddha given her by her friend Ida Baker. Here again the walls were covered with brown packing paper and the floor with matting. But it also contained a black grand piano and a black divan.

An evening or so later, after a 1/3d. dinner at the Dieppe restaurant, they were discussing where Murry should live. Katherine had already persuaded him to leave Oxford but he did not particularly want to stay with his family at Wandsworth. 'Why not my flat?' said Katherine. 'There's the Music Room. I hardly ever use it. We'll move the piano. Would seven-and-six a week be too much?' So on Thursday, 11 April 1912, he moved in and next morning on the kitchen table, found a large brown egg in an eggcup. Fixed between the egg and the eggcup was a half sheet of blue notepaper with the inscription: 'This is your egg. You must boil it. K.M.'

For the next four months the Buddha Room became the editorial office of *Rhythm*, the first magazine in England to publish drawings by Picasso. Murry had begun it at Oxford but was now – with the June number – able to expand it from a quarterly to a monthly. The strain on their finances, however, was such that some nights their dinner was a penny meat pie washed down with a beer at the Duke of York pub in Clerkenwell Road. There Len the landlord used to play *Rolling down to Rio* endlessly on the gramophone. Because of their unusual clothes – Murry favoured a blue fisherman's jersey, Katherine a black velvet jacket with orange scarf – Len's wife took them for an out-of-work music-hall act. 'I knew'd all along I seen yer on the 'alls,' she used to say.

For some time they lived in complete innocence but one evening Murry was musing on how long such happiness could last when Katherine said abruptly: 'Why don't you make me your mistress?' Murry's objection that it would 'spoil everything' was overcome by a traumatic experience they shared one night at the Duke of York's, when in the mirror behind the bar they saw reflected the eyes of Lil, the local prostitute. Her look of quiet desperation had the effect of throwing them straight into each other's arms.

Soon after that they had a visit from Katherine's husband, George Bowden, whom she had left the day after the wedding. He dropped in unexpectedly to ask what plans she had for divorcing. While considering the problem they persuaded him to sing some Schumann songs at the piano. Though he gave several encores, nothing definite was decided about a divorce. A more painful visit was that made by Murry's mother and aunt, who came to rescue him from temptation. It ended with a tug of war in the hall, with Murry finally closing the door on them shouting: 'Go away, you women, go away!' Happier was the time when the twenty-year-old sculptor Henri Gaudier came to dinner with his 'sister', Sophie Brzeska. Gaudier was especially delighted to learn that the Murrys were not married either: in fact, the Anglo-Slav entente became so rapturous that the stew was burnt and they had to make do with bread and cheese and coffee.

It was about this time that Murry received a monumental snub from Frank Harris at Dan Rider's bookshop, 36 St Martin's Court. He fled from the shop, pursued all the way back to the flat by Katherine crying, 'He'll kill himself, he'll kill himself!' Hugh Kingsmill found them weeping into the fire, after which Katherine went tearfully over to the window on Gray's Inn Road, saying: 'Oh wouldn't you love to be running by the sea with the sand trickling between your bare toes!'

A touching feature of the old Rate Books is that Katherine gives her name as 'Katerina'. It is a reminder of the pre-war Russian Ballet craze, when trendy ladies were all slightly Slav – even, it appears, to their rate man. Though 'Katerina's' name remains in the Rate Books until October 1912, it is doubtful if they ever lived in the flat after August, perhaps because neighbours began to look askance at their goings-on. Their hectic life together was transferred, first to a cottage near Chichester and then, in November, to rooms in Chancery Lane. It would be six years before they finally reached 'The Elephant', their famous house with the plaque in East Heath Road.

Charming Ghost

The other night in Mecklenburgh Square, WC1, 'deux formes ont tout à l'heure passé'. One was a sardonic gentleman looking vaguely like D. H. Lawrence, the other a beautiful dark girl called Dorothy ('Arabella') Yorke. From their clothes I guessed we were in the autumn of 1917. I thought I heard the purr of a zeppelin, but then a gust of laughter billowed forth from No. 44 (the home of Aldington and H.D.) where a jolly gathering was swapping gossip, or possibly partners. John Cournos had gone off to Russia to see the Revolution, leaving behind his friend Arabella. It was a mistake. Nothing in the house would ever be the same again, and Arabella was the charming catalyst.

At this very moment she was returning from dinner in Soho: 'They turned at last into the old, beautiful square. It seemed dark and deserted, dark like a savage wilderness in the heart of London. The wind was roaring in the great bare trees of the centre, as if it were some wild, dark grove deep in a forgotten land. She opened the gate of the Square garden with her key, and let it slam behind them . . . She led him across the grass to the big tree in the centre . . . They huddled against the big tree-trunk for shelter, and watched the scene. Beyond the tall shrubs and the high, heavy railings the wet street gleamed silently. The houses of the Square rose like a cliff on the inner dark sea, dimly lighted at occasional windows. Boughs swayed and sang . . .' (*Aaron's Rod*).

Meanwhile, in the Aldingtons' large, high, three-windowed sitting-room, with the apricot walls and the dark-blue curtains, there was a pause in the conversation. H. D. moved to the window and exclaimed in her sing-song voice, 'City of dreadful night, city of dreadful night!' She saw the railed-in square, the desolation of the empty street. It was a city of the dead. There were no lights visible in the block of walls that surrounded them; iron balconies gave on to the Square and the plane-trees stood stark metal.

Appropriately enough they all began talking about Arabella, the tall, slender, graceful girl with the black copper-tinged hair, brown eyes, high cheek bones and deep voice, originally discovered in America by Cournos. 'Her eyes at moments had the strangely attractive look of a hunted doe; it was as though she were frightened of life and expressed her innermost fear in occasional revealing moments' (Cournos in his *Autobiography*).

'She was the only dark one among us,' continued Brigit Patmore. 'She smouldered under her polished hair. She was cross because Lawrence compared her to a lacquer box, but she *was* imprisoned in something and disliked our prankiness' (*My Friends when Young*).

To Lawrence himself she was Josephine Ford in *Aaron's Rod*: 'a cameo girl with neat black hair done tight and bright in the French mode. She had strangely-drawn eyebrows, and her colour was brilliant . . . Her movements were very quiet and well bred; but perhaps too quiet . . . She smoked with short, sharp puffs . . . She had rather a stiff *poupée* walk . . . With her tight, black, bright hair, her arched brows, her dusky-ruddy face and her bare shoulders; her strange equanimity, her long, slow, slanting looks; she looked foreign and frightening, clear as a cameo, but dark, far off . . . She looked down with the fixed gravity of a Red Indian, immovable, inscrutable, then lifted her head, as if breaking a spell . . . He looked at the odd, round, dark muzzle of the girl . . . She folded her wrap around her, and hurried forward, with short, sharp steps. There was a certain Parisian *chic* and mincingness about her, even in her walk: but underneath, a striding, savage suggestion, as if she could leg it in great strides, like some squaw.'

To H. D., on the other hand, she was Bella Carter: 'Bella: foreign, exotic, bright parrot, a bird that talked . . . In spite of the wild-rose colour she had put on today to go with that green frock, she was oddly awkward, like a schoolgirl dressed up. She was tall, her feet were small, she moved with an awkward self-conscious gesture, like an animal tied up in clothes, pretty clothes. A deer, gazelle, with her tilted eyes, that looked out now as if she were suddenly frightened . . . Her hair combed tight back and varnished, her dark eyes pulled up at the corners were a mask, her words were rather toneless, she spoke in a voice that went with her marionette make-up . . . Why couldn't she keep her odalisque rôle, with her tight-pulled dark eyes and those two hairpins stuck in at the back of her long bob, which she had screwed up into a tight knot with those pins, stuck in at a perfect marionette angle?' (*Bid Me to Live*)

Dawn was breaking over the grey roof-tops but H. D. went on: 'Bella in her green dress, in the grey fitted one with buttons down the front, in the ultra-fashionable one with the wide pleated collar that made her (she wore white make-up for that) a girl-clown in a ballet. Ballet? It was *all ballet*.'

People and Places

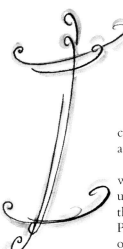 have mentioned my problem with Famous Men, but it is compounded with another: people for me have far less ambiance than places.

The film director Antonioni, for instance, evokes overwhelmingly for me a park in south-east London, which he used in *Blow-Up*. The sound of the wind rustling the trees that surrounded that curious little meadow on top of Maryon Park, Woolwich, haunts me still. And the mysterious letters of that neon sign which illuminates the scene later – it was an AEI sign down by the river *seen from the back*, I discovered, but the letters could have been Cyrillic – as enigmatic as the Oracle of Delphi. While other film-buffs argue intelligently about Antonioni's intentions, I keep going back to Maryon Park.

As a general rule I prefer films where real places are woven into the story. Carné's quite incidental treatment of the Bassin de la Villette in *Jenny* had me exploring the north-east of Paris for days on end. And if I still find those parts evocative today it has nothing to do with something that I discovered only later: that I'd been circling the site of the mediaeval gibbet of Montfaucon.

Even painters to me mean places. Samuel Palmer is that happy valley just off the M25 where the lighting is so theatrical that it *must* have been planned by God. And the name Matisse will always mean the façade of Notre-Dame seen from a certain angle: from the south-west to be precise. It was a view he painted from his studio on the quai Saint-Michel, but I saw it – over his shoulder, so to speak – from my sixth-floor room in the rue de la Huchette. It was my first room in Paris: to open your window in the morning and see Notre-Dame was sublime. Later I visited his famous flat with the aviary overlooking the Flower Market at Nice, but the painter I associate most with the Côte d'Azur is Bonnard.

It was the year of his big show at the Royal Academy, which contained views from all angles of the house at Le Cannet – including the bathroom where he endlessly painted his wife and model, the ageless Marthe. The house was then empty but, meeting his niece Aline Bowers by chance in a Cork Street gallery, I asked if I might visit it. She gave me full directions – 'You can climb over the garage' – but warned that I might find Arabs squatting. There were no Arabs there but I had to dash for my plane at Nice airport. None the less, when I think of Bonnard I can now place him fairly accurately in his background. And Marthe in her bath.

Cézanne was more elusive. I didn't feel his presence at all in the official studio at Aix, but one day I set out to find exactly from which spot he had painted the Pont de l'Arc. I was driving round with friends and we kept trying new roads and then reversing until at last we came to a private property. In the excitement of the chase we drove straight in and were congratulating ourselves on having found the spot – 'Look, this is that tree in the foreground' – when a touch on the shoulder made me turn and a lady informed me in the nicest way that we were trespassing. (The estate turned out to be Bellevue, where Cézanne had had a friend.)

Finally to the writers: there could hardly be a more evocative place in Paris than behind the altar of Saint-Sulpice, where the narrator meets God in Remy de Gourmont's marvellous *Une Nuit au Luxembourg*. That narrator was a journalist like me and, before entering the building, he had noted that the windows on the rue Palatine side of the church were illuminated as if by the setting sun; but there was no sun and, even if there had been, it would not have illuminated the south side at this late hour. It was, of course, the divine presence and later, after introducing himself, God invites the narrator to a night of philosophizing in the Luxembourg Garden, where I should very much like to have joined them. Just round the corner is Rilke's rue Toullier and his *Dame à la Licorne* in the Cluny Museum, equally evocative in their different ways.

When I first went to stay with a French family at Auteuil I was fifteen and my favourite place of meditation was the Pont Mirabeau, for I had read Apollinaire's poem of that name – it was a metaphor for being in love and I obligingly looked towards the lights of the Passy flats upstream where some elegant girl must surely be waiting. But by the time I went to Paris to work as a journalist and was ready to turn fantasy into action, I had learnt from Charles-Louis Philippe's *Bubu de Montparnasse* (which in these days of AIDS is probably due for a fresh lease of life) that there were darker sides to the enterprise. Even later an aura of horror hung around Philippe's name which was exorcized only after I'd spent a night in the house where he wrote the book (a hotel on the Ile Saint-Louis) and found I'd never slept better. After that I was ready for Henry Miller, who was certainly the American who best understood Paris, though the place he made most evocative for me was his own simple flat in Clichy suburb, beyond the outer boulevards, where he lived with Alfred Perlès, working 24 hours a day at being a writer.

During the war I was interned at Saint-Denis in the 18th century barracks of the old Swiss Guard, from the top floor of which we could see the not very evocative Eiffel Tower. One of the few consolations I found there was offered by a taboo periodical called *Je suis partout*. The Germans only let it in because it was a collaborationist rag, but one day it contained, surely by accident, Marcel Aymé's wonderful short story 'Avenue Junot'. I knew all about the avenue Junot, having lived in Montmartre. It was like going home, being with friends, writers and artists I'd known. A story of great warmth, dreamed up in difficult times . . . It would be excessive to say that 'Avenue Junot' saved my life, but I often raised a glass to it. And still do.

A Gentleman of France

efore the war, if you ever passed the famous Café de la Régence, which was situated at the south end of the avenue de l'Opéra, you might have seen, sitting in a chair on the terrace, a large man in a Canadian lumberjack's shirt and no jacket. If this man was also pulling contentedly on a rather rustic-looking pipe, then there is no doubt at all. He was Monier.

The Régence was one of the quieter, old-style cafés. Monier lived above it. Drinking rum in his flat, five flights up, I often felt a good deal higher than that. It was excellent rum and it came from his wife's relations in Martinique. It was better than you could buy in the rum café on the boulevard Saint-Germain.

From the balcony we used to survey the avenue de l'Opéra. We looked down on the Comédie-Française and watched the traffic all along the avenue as far as the Opera. Monier's life, though full and varied, was contained by this thoroughfare. He lived and worked here. And when he went for a walk he walked up the avenue.

Did he ever leave it? His friends would say no. He never went to the Rond-Point or Montparnasse to visit them: they had to come to him. And they always did, because Monier was *quelq'un*, Madame was *charmante* and the rum was *formidable*.

Sometimes as we stood up there Monier would say hard things about his avenue. He would call it the ugliest street in Paris. He would refer to the Opera, (away in the distance) and the Comédie (just below) as the National Tombs of Music and Drama. This meant nothing. He laughed at the things he loved, and when the time came he knew how to defend them with more than words. But at the moment there was no question of anyone defending the avenue de l'Opéra.

Monier was one of the mainstays of that lively weekly *Le Canard Enchaîné*, which might be inadequately translated as the *Captive Duck*. He was a big man who made tiny wistful drawings of donkeys and peasants. He also did old lady bigots and benign priests. Best of all were his cheerful birds and children. He had not always done little drawings. At one time they told him they would pay him by the inch, according to the area of newsprint he covered. So he made drawings of men with ladders. The captions would tell you what the man on top of the ladder said to the man at the bottom of the ladder. And the ladders got longer. After a few weeks they begged him to stop. They said they would pay him a flat rate per drawing, so he went back to the little drawings he loved. Besides being stylish and neat, they had a naïve, fairy-tale quality.

The *Captive Duck* was published from the offices of the big daily newspaper *L'Oeuvre* at the far end of the avenue near the Opera. I don't mean to suggest that Monier went to work in an office of the *Oeuvre* building. He simply went to the nearest bistro, which was called The Dial (*Le Cadran*). Leaning against the zinc counter with his colleagues he would talk over the happenings of the day until some humorous idea emerged. It was encouraged to emerge by an excellent little *vin blanc de Touraine* or maybe a Juliénas.

I doubt if any of the staff of the *Captive Duck* had offices of their own. The writers would correct and re-correct their proofs on the same zinc counter that served the artists as a drawing board. They were all rather like *enfants terribles* who had been sent to play in the street by old Grandfather *Oeuvre*.

The day after war broke out I happened to meet the 'man from the Gare Montparnasse'. This was a friend of Monier's and a rum-drinker like myself. Our rum-drinking, it seemed, was at an end. 'Il est parti ce matin'.

They'd taken Monier, a married man over forty who'd already served in the last war, and put him in the front line near Belfort. I did not know at the time that Daladier, who planned a war of passive defence in so far as he planned anything, had refused to put *young* Frenchmen on the frontier for fear they might get excited and provoke the Germans. As it happened Daladier did not expose my friend to any great risk except that of a slow death through boredom, but it did mean violent death to a lot of very pleasant habits. This big, friendly, check-shirted and rum-drinking man of the avenue de l'Opéra was removed from his avenue, his wife and his friends. In a dreary winter landscape he was condemned to play all day a card game called *belote*, and the people back in Paris called it the *drôle de guerre*.

One spring day of 1940 I met Monier on leave. It was before the German offensive. We didn't talk much about the war but I remember saying, 'I suppose Gamelin *is* the right man for the job?' Monier shrugged his broad shoulders: 'Tu crois qu'il en sait plus long que nous? And even if he were a genius, would it make any difference?' I thought Monier had just grown stale with the months of waiting, but he was soon proved right. After Pétain's armistice he was faced with a dilemma which he resolved characteristically.

He reasoned thus: 'The French Press is now controlled by Germany. By having anything to do with it I work for Germany. Therefore I will have nothing to do with it. Instead, I will illustrate the fables of La Fontaine for French schoolchildren.'

There were not many such anti-collaborationists. Even the most enlightened people allowed their plays and films to be applauded by German officers. It would have been easy for Monier to find a niche in some paper or other for his funny little drawings which, after all, were never greatly concerned with politics. But he preferred to make a complete break, and in the end he was rewarded. The childlike drawings burst freshly on Paris after the Liberation because they had never been associated with the German interlude. Monier became a symbol of Paris reborn. The new papers clamoured for his work, papers like *Carrefour* and *Lettres Françaises*, as well, of course, as the liberated *Captive Duck* itself.

When the Germans entered Paris the *Duck* had ceased publication, while its big brother *L'Oeuvre* became prosperous under the direction of the notorious pro-German Marcel Déat. After the Liberation *L'Oeuvre* died the death of a traitor and the little *Duck* rose phoenix-like from its own ashes.

The waiting years, however, had been lean ones for Monier. There is not much money in illustrating the fables of La Fontaine. When Monier came to see me in the internment camp I noticed with a pang that his lumberjack's shirt was pretty threadbare. 'I haven't brought you any rum,' he said. 'We don't drink it any more. Bad for the stomach.' A great gust of laughter surprised the other visitors and internees around us. Monier laughed like some large good-natured animal in a Walt Disney film. Even the German guard behind us couldn't resist that laugh, but Monier turned on him. 'What have *you* got to laugh about?' The guard, a Bavarian peasant who knew no French, nodded and grinned sheepishly.

But all this only leads up to the great day, the apotheosis of Monier, when he helped to defend his beloved avenue de l'Opéra. I don't know if Mme Monier saw it from the balcony. I wasn't there, and yet I see the whole scene very clearly.

I can see Monier in a red-and-green check shirt helping to build the barricade with paving stones and iron grids from the bases of the trees. I can see him waiting for action, side by side with the man from the Gare Montparnasse. I can see France's foremost *soubrette* encouraging them with hot coffee, while a member of the Opera orchestra arrives down from Montmartre with a Sten gun in his violin case.

I can see spent bullets shattering the plate-glass of the Régence and startling the older clients. I can hear Monier's deep chuckle as he fixes to the front of the barricade a poster representing Marcel Déat, pro-German director of *L'Oeuvre*. And I can feel his deep satisfaction when the Nazi tank-gunners blow Marcel Déat to pieces but do not pass up the avenue de l'Opéra.

Tale of a Tree

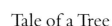

I t was a sort of endless chant that the children were singing as they paraded round the little town: 'For Mary who spreads the fields with flowers, who fills the fishermen's nets and weighs down the olive trees . . . give, give, give.' I had arrived in Cassis the previous night, after a twelve-hour journey from Paris, so I wasn't too pleased to be woken at 6 a.m., even by children singing.

But after a bit I went down and gave my francs for Mary, at the same time admiring the mountains of flowers which were being borne around on little platforms in her honour. I asked one of the girls where I could go for a walk before breakfast. She suggested along the rocks to the Pointe du Château and then slip down into the bay the other side. Afterwards I could climb up to the route de l'Arène and so back to the hotel.

I don't suppose anyone appreciates the south of France so much as an Englishman on the morning of his arrival. From the moment your bare feet touch the tiled floor of your bedroom and you hear the tinny sound of church bells your heart feels somehow lighter. And when you go down to the luminous little port with the white boats dancing, you know what it means, that phrase about walking on air.

I followed the directions and climbed those rocks which, by some miracle, were a mass of valerian and genista. This in itself was a surprise because I had always associated valerian with Cotswold stone walls. I had never been south in May before. Expecting morning glories I found valerian and felt rather cheated. It's true that this was the most luxuriant valerian you could imagine, and the genista flowers with their sweet, fresh smell were the biggest I had ever seen, but these were poor compensations. Even when I learnt – as I did later – that valerian was known in these parts as *lilas sauvage*, wild lilac – and in patois *ivrogne*, drunkard – even then it still looked like valerian.

I slipped down into the bay, just as my guide had recommended, and by this time I was beginning to think of those hot *brioches*, joy of French breakfasts. So, when I began the steep ascent to the route de l'Arène I had one thing in mind – to get back to the hotel as quickly as possible, and enough of this admiring nature on an empty stomach.

I think it was the unexpectedness of it that took my breath away. The path I was climbing was made of loose stones which began slipping as soon as you trod on them: you had to keep a grip all the time on some overhanging branch or one of the tough little bushes that grew alongside. I was absorbed in not crashing down into the blue Mediterranean when suddenly I became aware of an overpowering scent heavy in the air about me. Only some semi-tropical tree with great waxen flowers could match a scent like that. I looked for one but there was nothing in sight. Puzzled, I climbed to the top of the cliff where the path joins the route de l'Aréne. Just at the top there is a pleasant farmhouse called the 'Clos de la Madeleine' where some of the best Cassis wine is produced. That's on the right, while on the left is a garden wall. I was walking by this wall when I saw it.

How does one describe a tree when one isn't an expert? In some ways it was like an *olivier* which had shaken off that centuries-old look and gone berserk. The leaves seemed to be silver on *both* sides, and the flowers which hung in tumbling clusters were bright yellow. It had the elegance of an acacia and the lush abandon of a weeping willow. I was able to break off a branch to smell the blossom because the tree, though rooted in a private garden, overhung the path. The smell was almost of pineapple.

For the next day or so I carried my branch around and I think I must have asked about twenty people what it was. None of them knew, and not until the eve of my departure did I see another like it. That was in the garden of the *mairie* and, as there was a knowledgeable-looking concierge type standing by, I seized the opportunity, 'Madame, comment s'appelle cette arbre là?' 'B'en quoi, c'est un olivier de Bohême,' she replied, as if surprised that anyone could be so ignorant.

Olivier de Bohême. So I had not been so far wrong when I compared it to a young, light-hearted olive tree. It was the gypsy among olives – careless, abandoned.

When I got back to England I found I was thinking more and more of my tree. By now, of course, it was more than a tree: it stood for Cassis, the tiled floor, the children singing and much else besides. Dreaming of a tree is all very well but one day I decided to possess it. I wrote to the Royal Horticultural Society who said: 'Olivier de Bohême is a French vernacular name for Elaeagnus angustifolia, a tree that has been in cultivation in England for about three centuries.' This was good news, so I wrote to various nurserymen, one of whom promised me my tree, in a pot, for autumn delivery.

It came last October and has survived the winter. There it grows, the almost legendary *olivier de Bohême* – marvel of Cassis – in the shade of a Cotswold wall. Visitors, I find, are unimpressed; they don't seem to see its matchless beauty of form and colour, the yellow flowers caught in a cascade of silvery leaves, and the overpowering perfume. They see only a stringy root nine inches high.

Poets at Play

Welcomed into the bosom of the French Academy on 30 May 1895, the Parnassian poet José-Maria de Heredia (*Les Trophées*) was perhaps even better known for his three beautiful daughters: Hélène, Marie and Louise, of whom the most beautiful was Marie. Thanks to the revelations of a French magazine we have heard much of Marie lately.

The Heredia family was of Cuban origin, which gave the girls a dark and piquant charm that Paris found irresistible. But Marie was as witty and intelligent as she was beautiful. While still in her teens she was a regular contributor of poems to the *Revue des Deux Mondes* under the intriguing pen-name of★★★; and a month after her father became Academician she formed her own academy – the Académie Canaque or Canaquadémie – for admission to which candidates were required only to make 'grimaces artistiques'. Yet the membership was hardly less brilliant than that of the real Academy, including as it did the young Paul Valéry and (as perpetual secretary) a certain Marcel Proust.

Marie had, of course, many suitors, of whom the frontrunners were two up-and-coming poets: Henri de Régnier (*Tel qu'en songe*) and Pierre Louÿs (*Les Chansons de Bilitis*). Both could be described as dandies but, while Henri was rich and aloof (his nickname was the English 'Stick'), Pierre was relatively poor and much more likeable: he had been widely recognized as 'mon grand ami Hubert' in Gide's brilliant *Paludes*, published earlier that year.

Henri (30) and Pierre (25) had a gentleman's agreement that they would inform each other of their intentions towards Marie (20) – but on 13 July Henri apparently broke the agreement by announcing his engagement. It was said that he had agreed to pay all Heredia's gambling debts: in other words the marriage had been 'arranged'. Pierre and Marie never forgave him; for the latter indeed it was especially mortifying: a feminist many years before her time it was Marie who proclaimed: 'Girls today are like houses, of which the freehold is up for sale but letting is forbidden. Clients may occasionally inspect the premises but certainly not all floors.'

On 15 July Pierre wrote to the old man: 'Monsieur, I adored your daughter, though I never told her so: for years I dreamed of marrying her when I could offer her something more than a poor man's purse and an unknown name. Today I realize that I have been forestalled and that my hopes are dashed. Be so good as to forgive me if I lack the courage ever to return to a house in which I received always the most affectionate welcome but which I could not re-enter without tears.' Three days later the old man called on Pierre, attempting to explain, and before leaving offered him six cherrywood pipes for only 40 centimes each. Reporting this to his brother, Pierre wrote: 'That's him all over, he's unique and absurd! How can you be angry with a man like that!'

So the marriage duly took place, though Pierre very pointedly did not attend. It was some eighteen months later, in fact, that he reappeared, having set up home in the boulevard Malesherbes with a North African girl called Zohra. It was transparently an effort to forget Marie, who seems to have been so stung by the move that she flew straight into Pierre's arms. On 17 October 1897 (an historic date) Pierre and Mouche (as he called her) began their famous 'noces mystérieuses' in a specially rented apartment in the avenue Carnot. It was one of the most celebrated liaisons of the time, throughout which 'Stick' remained the long-suffering and always polite third man. By January Marie was pregnant, at which Pierre retired in confusion, being undecided what to do next. Indecision was his second name and usually involved his retiring to North Africa to think things out (a habit later to be adopted by Henry de Montherlant in his skirmishes with *les jeunes filles*).

The baby was born on 8 September 1898 and christened Pierre, which suggested to Pierre Louÿs that he might have been forgiven, as did the fact that he was chosen as godfather. To make quite sure he put a coded advertisement in the *Echo de Paris* saying: 'Never forget 17 October 1897. Do you forgive me?' This appeared on 28 October 1898 at the beginning of a weekend that Marie had planned for all three of them in Amsterdam. At one of the stations en route, 'Stick' having alighted to go in search of refreshments, Marie leant across the carriage to Pierre and whispered 'Bonjour!' After this, she behaved to 'Stick' so abominably that Pierre was almost sorry for his rival: in his own words, 'Marie acted like the people of a turbulent country who have warned their king once and for all to let them be, or get the hell out.'

Despite Pierre's qualms there was apparently no stopping the two poets' passionate devotion to one another, which eventually reached its climax in another historic date in the avenue Carnot: 29 November 1898, which Pierre immortalized in his poem 'L'Apogée' ('The Zenith'), itself to become an integral part of the longer poem *Pervigilium Mortis*. Their love had reached its highest flight, after which it was bound to descend (weighted not a little by Pierre's indecision). Alone in the avenue Carnot flat the following February, Marie wrote a poem of her own: the 'Epigraphe' which is reminiscent of Ronsard and which many people (Pierre Louÿs among them) have preferred to 'L'Apogée'.

In the period of anti-climax that followed Pierre could think of nothing better to do than marry Marie's sister Louise, a decision which that indecisive man was to describe as 'the ultimate stupidity for which I feel not merely regret but remorse.' Years later in a wry quote from *Antony and Cleopatra* he wrote to Mouche: 'We have kiss'd away kingdoms and provinces – though all we had to lose (and lost) was each other.'

INDEX

Italic type indicates illustrations